Thermal Delight in Architecture

Lisa Heschong

Thermal Delight in Architecture

The MIT Press

Cambridge, Massachusetts

and

London, England

This book was set in VIP Meridien
by Achorn Graphic Services, Inc.,
printed and bound
in the United States of America

Library of Congress Cataloging in Publication Data

Heschong, Lisa.
    Thermal Delight in Architecture.

    1. Architecture and climate.
    2. Vernacular architecture.
    I. Title.
NA2541.H47   720'.1   79–20492
ISBN 978-0-262-08101-6 (hardcover: alk. paper)
ISBN 978-0-262-58039-7 (paperback)

20 19 18

Contents

Preface   vii

Acknowledgments   xi

Necessity   1

Delight   18

Affection   31

Sacredness   50

Notes   73

Preface

This work began with the hypothesis that the thermal function of a building could be used as an effective element of design. Thermal qualities—warm, cool, humid, airy, radiant, cozy—are an important part of our experience of a space; they not only influence what we choose to do there but also how we feel about the space. An analogy might be drawn with the use of light quality as a design element, truly a venerable old architectural tradition. The light quality—direct, indirect, natural, artificial, diffuse, dappled, focused—can be subtly manipulated in the design of a space to achieve the desired effect. Thermal qualities might also be included in the architect's initial conception and could influence all phases of design. Instead, thermal conditions are commonly standardized with the use of modern mechanical systems that can be specified, installed, and left to function independently of the overall design concept. Indeed, environmental control systems tend to be treated rather like the Cinderella of architecture; given only the plainest clothes to wear, they are relegated to a back room to do the drudgery that maintains the elegant life-style of the other sisters: light, form, structure, and so forth.

I became intrigued with the design potential of thermal qualities when I was working on the design of a solar building. Rather than simply housing an autonomous mechanical system, the building itself acted as the thermal system. The living room was both for living in and for collecting heat. The south windows allowed a view and also let in the warmth of the winter sun. Thermal shutters, closed at night, made the house more introverted while also saving heat. I began to wonder how the thermal qualities of this building affected peoples' experience of it. I realized that there were very few references on which to draw. The one obvious analogy was the fireplace. The solar-heating functions of the building were essentially a replacement of the original thermal functions of the fireplace. With its circle of warmth, the fireplace had once been the center of family life. Its dancing light, smoky smells, and warm crackling created an ambience that made a house more a home. And the traditions around the hearth stretched back through the ages, connecting each house to deep cultural roots. How might the solar house incorporate some of the richness of the hearth? What were the qualities of the hearth that made it so wonderful and so beloved?

I decided to look not only at hearths but at places with strong thermal qualities from a broad spectrum of cultures and historical periods, with the assumption that there was a universality of human experience that might be distilled from them. I have looked at the examples not with the eye of a historian (How did it come to be?) or of an engineer (How does it work?) but rather with the eye of a designer

(How is it perceived? What role does it play in peoples' lives? What is wonderful about it? How is it part of a greater whole?). Unfortunately, information on peoples' actual use and experience of places tends to be sparse. It is perhaps a sad commentary on the state of architectural literature that so little attention is paid to how people ultimately use spaces and what they feel about them. The most illuminating descriptions are often written by anthropologists, literary travelers, or poets.

Other than the hearth, perhaps the richest example of a thermal place with a profound role in its culture is the Islamic garden, the cool oasis that is the traditional center of the Islamic house. Together they might be regarded as two archetypes: the hearth, a refuge of dry warmth from a cold world, and the oasis, a preserve of coolness and moisture in a desert wilderness.

It is hoped that this collection of disparate examples may serve as a set of references for the designer. It draws no firm conclusions and sets no guidelines; rather, it offers some background information and a bit of musing, which are the first stages of any design work.

Acknowledgments

The thinking and caring of many people has been woven into this book. Their contributions, whether knowing or not, have greatly enriched its fabric. Douglas Mahone, my dear friend and constant consultant, kept me afloat in the roughest waters with his steadfast encouragement. The clear and critical thinking of Edward Allen and Lynn Parisi contributed greatly to the organization and coherence of the writing. Many people helped in one way or another with the research for this book: Seleh-Ali Al-hathlool, Bruce Anderson, Dolores Hayden, Timothy Johnson, P. T. Krishnan, Tunny Lee, Noriko Nishizawa, Gunter Nitschke, Henry Millon, Kalev Ruberg, Robert Slattery, Eleanor and Robert Templeton, Sean Wellesley-Miller, Jennifer Young. A generous fellowship from the American Association of University Women partially supported the work.

Passages from the following works are quoted in this volume by permission of the authors, their publishers, or their agents:

The Psychoanalysis of Fire
by Gaston Bachelard,
published by Beacon Press, 1964.

Thermal Delight in Architecture

Necessity

Life exists within a small range of temperatures. It comes to a standstill as water freezes and even the hardiest of bacteria are destroyed in boiling water. Each species of plant or animal has definite limits within which it can survive and an even narrower range of temperatures where it can successfully compete with other animals. Ecologists have discovered that as little as a 2°F change in the average temperature of a lake will shift the dominant fish population from bass to catfish as one species becomes more efficient than the other. Thus, not only extremes but even subtle variations in temperature can be critical to an animal's survival.

The oceans, where life evolved, provide a particularly stable thermal environment where organisms can live without much thermal stress. Fish and other cold-blooded sea creatures can function perfectly well at the temperature of their watery environment because the temperature of the ocean, and thus of their bodies, varies so little, and then only very gradually. The land, however, experiences great swings of temperature. The surface of the earth is constantly heating up and cooling down with each daily cycle and each yearly cycle. The ground, in turn, heats the air around it, driving the forces of weather that can so dramatically change thermal conditions over the course of a few hours. In order to move out of the oceans and onto the land, organisms had to develop thermal strategies that would allow them to survive both climatic extremes and wide daily fluctuations.

The most direct way to cope with an adverse climate is simply to not be there when it gets too hot or too cold. Many of the simpler forms of life, such as bacteria, fungi, and yeast, stop metabolizing—essentially stop living—when the temperature becomes inhospitable. Yeast can be stored in a refrigerator almost indefinitely. Put it back into 90°F water and it comes most prolifically alive. Many plants and insects solve the problem similarly. They live only during the most favorable season; then before dying off, they leave seeds or eggs behind that will sprout or hatch only when the next good season arrives.

If, however, an individual is to survive through a yearly cycle of seasons, it must employ some thermal strategy more sophisticated than simply not being there. One way not to be there, without dying, is to be deciduous, a strategy employed by plants not only in snowy climates but in desert climates as well. By dropping all of their leaves, they reduce their exposure to temperature extremes. Metabolic activity continues, but at a greatly reduced level, withdrawing to a protected core or to roots sheltered underground. Cold-blooded animals and a few of the smallest mammals have a similar strategy to deal with extreme cold: they hibernate. The metabolic rate of a cold-blooded animal, or any organism for that matter, is closely tied to the temperature of its body. As its temperature rises, it becomes more active, and as its temperature falls, it becomes sluggish and lethargic. When the environmental temperature becomes too cold, cold-blooded animals simply give up the effort to function and go into hibernation. Like deciduous plants, they retreat to a place sheltered from temperature extremes, a nest underground or within the insulating wood of a tree. As the body temperature drops, the metabolic rate is greatly reduced, enabling the animal to conserve energy for survival through the dormant period.

Animals have a great thermal advantage over plants because they can move about. Rather than endure the thermal conditions of one place, they can choose the most favorable location. Good travelers, such as birds and large herd mammals, can migrate between entire climatic zones so that they never have to endure the worst of any particular region. Migration is a way not to be there without a seasonal pause in activity. On a smaller scale, animals can also move about to take advantage of the variations in climate that occur within a given landscape. The slope of a hill that faces the sun or is sheltered from a cold wind will be warmer than the opposite slope. Indeed, this variation in microclimate can be so significant that entirely different communities of plants will grow on the opposite sides of a hill, each community thriving in the climate to which it is best adapted. An animal, on the other hand, can select among the various microclimates according to its needs. Snakes, sluggish from the night's cold, will crawl out of their holes to bask in the morning sun. With the sun's heat they can raise their body temperature considerably and begin to function effectively even though the morning air may still be quite cold.

Indeed, cold-blooded animals have surprising abilities to maintain a steady body temperature in spite of swings in the external temperature. Terrestrial cold-blooded animals, unlike fish, are not completely at the mercy of their thermal environment. In addition to moving to the best thermal location, they can also wilfully vary their muscular activity to generate more heat within their bodies. On a cold day butterflies will vibrate their wings for several minutes to warm their muscles enough so that they can fly. Lizards can maintain a body temperature to within 1°F of their optimum by combining these two strategies: to warm up, they do "push-ups" on a sunny rock; to cool down, they retreat to a shady crevice and lie still.

It is the genius of the warm-blooded animals, the birds and the mammals, that they evolved with a system for regulating their internal body temperature that takes full advantage of the heat naturally generated by their metabolism. Mammals have refined the muscular

3

heat-generating technique of the cold-blooded animals so that a change in muscle tone can produce subtle gradations in the amount of body heat produced. Vibrations of the muscles have become an automatic shivering response as an emergency heat-generating measure. Over longer periods of time many mammals can actually raise their basal metabolic rate to acclimate to cold.

Even more significant than the ability to change the rate of heat production is the capability of warm-blooded animals to regulate the rate of heat flow away from their bodies. Although all animals generate heat from their metabolism, only the warm-blooded animals can control how fast their heat is lost. They have a variety of mechanisms that allow them either to release their excess heat into the environment to stay cool or to so thoroughly insulate themselves that their body heat is retained even in the coldest of places. Panting or sweating creates evaporative cooling from the mouth or skin. Birds do not have the ability to sweat, so on a hot day one is likely to find them splashing in a puddle or bird bath, cooled by the water's evaporation.

One of the most important ways to regulate the flow of heat is through the circulation of the blood. Mammals and birds can control how much blood is flowing to the surface of their skin, even to entire extremities. By flushing the skin with blood, the heat of the inner body is pumped to the surface where it can readily escape. Conversely, by restricting the flow of blood to the surface, the blood's heat is retained in the animal's inner core. Many waterfowl can cut off most all blood flow to their legs in order to reduce the heat lost to the cold water.

Mammals and birds have also developed a marvelous variety of ways to insulate their bodies. Fat, which occurs in other animals only as lumps that store food energy, is deployed in many mammals as a special insulating layer under the skin. Its thickness varies in response to seasonal demands for protection against extra cold. Polar bears and husky dogs have such an effective layer of fat that they can comfortably sleep on ice. Human beings, too, have this subcutaneous fat that can thicken in response to cold. Fur or feathers provide another type of insulation, one that is exquisitely variable. Over the course of a year it can change in quality, quantity, even color. Smooth and sleek and a bit oily in the summer, fur or feathers protect the owner's skin from the sun's hot rays. In winter an extra downy undercoat is grown that can be fluffed up at a moment's notice to provide an even thicker, more effective insulation. Getting goosebumps when we are suddenly chilled is a remnant of response from the time when our ancestors still had fur to fluff. A coat of fur or feathers essentially traps a bubble of air that has its own climatic conditions; the animal's skin is exposed not to the prevailing climate but to the warmer air contained within the downy fur.

When in the course of evolution human beings lost the thick mammalian fur coat, they also lost its capabilities for thermal control. Our naked skin functions adequately in the hot, humid tropics but needs some assistance in other climates. The traditional clothing developed by various cultures often has extremely sophisticated thermal functions. The billowing white robes of the Arab reflect away the sun's radiation while helping to fan air past the body and increase evaporative cooling. At the other extreme, the fur parka of the Eskimo keeps in both body heat and water vapor from perspiration so that the Eskimo essentially lives within a semitropical environment.

Of all the creatures, human beings have the greatest variety of thermal strategies available to them. Our mammalian heritage gives us metabolic adjustments that allow us to maintain comfort over quite a spread of thermal conditions. In addition to this ability for metabolic fine tuning, we have other strategies available to us. Like the lizard and butterfly, we can consciously vary our muscular activity to increase or decrease heat production. Rubbing your hands together or stomping up and down brings immediate results when you need to warm up. Such thermal responses have even developed into regional patterns. In hot climates the cool morning is usually the time of most activity, whereas during the hot afternoon everything slows down. Siesta time ensures that people's own heat production will be kept to a minimum during the hottest part of the day.

A human parallel to long animal migrations can be seen in the common tradition of a special summer place. The British in India simply packed up during the hottest months and moved business, the colonial government, and all social life up to hill stations, towns in the Himalayan foothills where the air was cooler. Similarly, New Englanders have a strong tradition of summer cottages. Many families maintain a cottage somewhere in the country or along the seacoast where on weekend visits or for a whole summer's vacation they find relief from the hot city and delight in the pleasures of the countryside. Wealthy families often extend this migration system to include a midwinter trip to Miami or the Bahamas to escape the bitter January cold.

Migration, however, is an expensive solution, whether in terms of the energy an animal must use to travel long distances or the time and money that people must spend. And before cars, trains, and airplanes, human migration was extremely slow. Preindustrial people could not travel very quickly, especially when moving a household. Ralph Knowles gives a good description of the seasonal migrations of the Piute Indians of the Owens Valley in California. Note that the total distance traveled is only thirty miles round trip:

> From permanent settlements, generally located in the
> most favorable microclimate, including a good water
> supply, the Piutes made seasonal migrations as village
> groups. Each summer, as the days began to lengthen

and the temperature began to climb, the group moved west into the higher meadows of the Sierras. Here they enjoyed the coolness of an increased elevation. As the fall approached and passed into early winter, they migrated ten to fifteen miles to the east, where they gathered pine nuts at the base of the White Mountains. Here they were at a lower elevation and had a west and somewhat south exposure adding to their comfort as the winter days approached. The seasonal cycle was finally completed when they returned to their permanent campsite at the base of the Sierras to live out the winter in the relative comfort of huts that could be heated fairly well.[1]

Nest building is, in a way, a more advanced version of choosing the best microclimate. An animal seeking out a rock crevice or hole in the earth as a place to rest and be cool is indeed seeking out a favorable microclimate. Digging the hole a little deeper and adding a bit of shed fur for insulation are simple improvements. All animals start their nests by finding the best location and only a few of the most talented nest builders—such as some birds, beavers, and Homo sapiens—can completely transform an environment to meet their nesting needs. The Anasazi Indians of the southwestern United States were remarkably clever in choosing the sites for their cliff dwellings. They invariably chose locations shaded in the summer by an overhanging ledge of the cliff, but exposed to full sun all winter long. With their backs to the cliff, the dwellings were protected from the winter winds and also took advantage of the thermal mass of the earth to moderate the temperature flux.

Buildings, even in the conventional ways we now build them, can be viewed as a way to modify a landscape to create more favorable microclimates. As soon as a simple square hut is built, at least six new microclimates are created: the south side warmed by a sunny wall, the north side in shade most of the time, an east side with its morning sun and perhaps protected from the prevailing breeze, and a west side warmed in the afternoon but buffeted by the wind. There is also the inside with its shelter from the rain and wind and sun, and the roof, raised above ground level, more exposed to wind and sun. A building increases the available range of thermal zones so that people can select the microclimate most suited to their thermal needs.

Many peoples of North Africa migrate within their buildings in both daily and seasonal patterns to take advantage of the various microclimates the buildings create. In Tunisia, for example, the traditional two-story house encloses a central courtyard with colonnades along all sides. In the summer when the sun is high, the colonnade creates a deep shade. The family spends the day in the interior rooms of the first floor where the thermal mass of the building best protects them from the sun's heat. At night they move out onto the open roof, which quickly loses its heat to the clear night sky. In the wintertime the pattern is reversed. The family members spend their days on the roof and the upper loggia where the winter sun can still reach to warm them. At night they retreat to the rooms of the upper story, whose walls have retained some of the heat from the day's sun, where they can take advantage of any heat rising from below.

Vernacular building traditions all over the world display remarkably sophisticated thermal adaptation. Primitive builders consistently used forms and materials that effectively moderated prevailing climatic conditions. In the desert the characteristic problem is extremely high daytime temperatures coupled with uncomfortably low temperatures at night. The ideal building material would have a high heat capacity in order to absorb solar radiation during the day and slowly reradiate it at night. "Clay and stone are high heat capacity materials; they are plentiful in the desert, and it is precisely out of them that primitive folk around the world make their buildings," writes James Marston Fitch in an article on "Primitive Architecture and Climate."[2] Buildings of adobe, mud and rubble masonry, and thick clay mortar on twig mesh are found in the American southwest, in the Middle East, and across Africa from the Nile delta to the Gold Coast. Conversely, primitive peoples in the hot, humid tropics built dwellings that reduced thermal mass to a minimum using light materials such as bamboo and reeds to avoid significant reradiation of heat. Ventilation was maximized to increase the potential for evaporative cooling by placing large openings in the walls or by eliminating walls altogether. Large roofs provided shade and shelter from the rains. Such dwellings can be found throughout the South Pacific, the Caribbean, and among the Seminole Indians of Florida. This was also the basic approach of the Japanese in coping with their humid summers; it led to the classic Japanese house, with its great sheltering roof and removable paper walls.

A particularly ingenious response to climatic needs is seen in the Eskimo igloo. Fitch analyzes the most important features of the igloo's thermal performance:

> [The igloos's] hemispherical dome offers the maximum resistance and the minimum obstruction to winter gales, and at the same time exposes the least surface to their chilling effect. The dome has the further merits of enclosing the largest volume with the

smallest structure; at the same time it yields that volume most effectively heated by the point source of radiant heat afforded by an oil lamp.

The intense and steady cold of the Arctic dictates a wall material of the lowest possible heat capacity; dry snow meets this criterion admirably, though at first glance it seems the least likely structural material imaginable. . . . The insulating value of this shell is further improved by a glaze of ice that the heat of an oil lamp and the bodies of occupants automatically add to the inner surface. This ice film seals the tiny pores in the shell and, like the aluminum foil on the inner face of modern wall insulation, acts as a radiant-heat reflector. When, finally, the Eskimo drapes the interior of his snow shell with skins and furs, thereby preventing the chilling of his body by either radiant or conductive heat loss to the cold floor and walls, he has completed an almost perfect instrument of control of his thermal environment.[3]

Clever use of the insulating qualities of snow is not unique to the human inhabitants of the arctic. Many arctic animals make their nests buried deep in the snow where, protected from the winds, their body heat can warm the enclosure. But the Eskimo has one transcendant advantage—the use of fire.

The use of fire offers enormous potential to affect the thermal environment. Plants and the simpler animals are totally dependent upon the sun and weather to provide the heat necessary for their survival. Cold-blooded animals begin to make use of their own body heat to help keep themselves warm, and the warm-blooded animals are masters at regulating this internal source. Fire allows human beings a third mechanism, one independent of the fluctuations of climate and their own metabolism. With the control of fire, people can generate heat at will to warm themselves and their environment. The Eskimo's oil lamp is a considerable refinement of the primitive campfire—cleaner, smaller, more efficient, and portable. To fire, we have added other sources of energy, such as electricity, to power equipment that has given us ever more precise control over the thermal environment. Fascination with this potential for control of our environment has prompted the invention of mechanical systems that have made natural thermal strategies seem obsolete by comparison.

Histories of civilization often begin with the discovery of fire. There seems to be a general belief in the civilizing force of the warmth of fire, such as inspired Vitruvius to write,

> The men of old were born like wild beasts, in woods, caves, and groves, and lived on savage fare. As time went on, the thickly crowded trees in a certain place, tossed by storms and winds, and rubbing their branches against one another, caught fire, and so the inhabitants of the place were put to flight, being terrified of the flames. After it subsided, they drew near, and observing that they were comfortable standing before a warm fire, they put logs on and

while keeping it alive, brought other people to it, showing them by signs how much comfort they got from it. . . . Therefore it was the discovery of fire that originally gave rise to the coming together of men, to the deliberative assembly, and to social intercourse."[4]

The use of fire as a heat source, however, might originally have been quite secondary to its other uses: as a way to prepare and cook food; as a way to smoke out pests and discourage predators; and on the most primal level, as a focus of mystical fascination. Warm and glowing like a little piece of the sun, growing, moving, and dying like some bodiless spirit, the fire seemed to have magical properties. It has been hypothesized that some of the first efforts at building were attempts to shelter the sacred fire from rain and wind.

Indeed, the most primitive dwelling of many cultures was typically just a small round shelter with a firepit at its center, little more than a campfire within an enclosure. In Europe, as late as the Middle Ages, it was still common practice to have an open fire in the center of a room with the smoke escaping out a hole in the roof gable. Such fireplaces were enormously inefficient, causing as many heating problems as they solved. Flames were more valued than embers, but the large open fires consumed great quantities of oxygen, pulling the cold outside air in through the cracks of the building as quickly as the heated air escaped up the chimney hole. Since the air inside the dwelling would not stay heated, the only way to benefit from the fire's warmth was to sit directly in front of the flames to absorb its thermal radiation. Thus, our ancestors could only enjoy the heat of a fire when there were sedentary activities or cooking to be done. The rest of the time they had to depend upon heavy clothes and their own energy to keep them warm.

Around the end of the Middle Ages the notion of a chimney to channel off the smoke of the fire began to take hold. Unfortunately, it was learned only by trial and error that the chimney needed to be made of fireproof materials. After many disastrous fires, towns began to institute laws forbidding the use of wooden chimneys. People soon realized that a stone or brick chimney not only was safer but also absorbed heat from the fire and later reradiated it back into the room. To take advantage of this form of heat storage, people began to build ever more massive masonry chimneys. In homes in northern Europe, these chimneys evolved into a huge central mass that might incorporate a number of fireplaces, ovens, and flues, with a sleeping loft on top where a bed could be kept deliciously warm.

When firewood began to become scarce, however, people looked for a heating system that would be more efficient than an open fire. England effectively ran out of wood for fires in the 1600s, as the forests were appropriated for ship building and making charcoal for metallurgy. But the English were exceptionally fond of their open hearths and reluctant to change to the more efficient system of coal fires and closed stoves that were already in use on the continent. They persisted in using fireplaces, even though improvements in their efficiency were made only gradually.

The greatest impetus for improvement came from the United States in the eighteenth century. Count Rumford endeavored to make a science of fireplace efficiency. He designed a fireplace that radiated a much greater percentage of its heat out into the room. Benjamin Franklin had an even better idea. He enclosed the fire in a metal box to control the rate of combustion and to separate the combustion gases from the surrounding air and then moved it out into the middle of the room where its heat could radiate in all directions. The Franklin stove was the "Model T" of the heating business, mass produced and the pride of households all over the country.

The Franklin stove also brought with it the revolutionary idea that a fire could heat a house indirectly by heating the air, which could then be circulated to keep people warm anywhere in the house. Its use initiated the changeover from a radiant to a convective system of heating. Improvements were made to extract more and more heat from the fire box, and the stove was transformed into a furnace. For the first time people began to understand a building as an enclosure for a bubble of warmed air and realized that attention had to be paid to making the building more airtight. Simply blocking out the rain and wind isn't sufficient in an air-heated house, for if a building still leaks air, pressure from the wind can drive all of the heated air to one side of the house and out through the walls.

The new scientific understanding of the processes of convection and radiation brought a flurry of effort to design the perfect furnace—safe, clean, efficient, and inexpensive. At first, natural or gravity convection was most commonly used to move the warmed air through the house, but pressure differentials and temperature stratification tended to create a very uneven distribution of heat. Steam heat looked promising for a while because it solved the problem of moving the heat from where the fuel burned to where it was actually wanted. The steam could be piped under its own pressure and then, on losing its heat, would condense back to water and return by gravity. Steam radiators, however, were noisy and excessively hot. With the development of small electric motors, heat distribution problems were more easily and comfortably solved. Small electric pumps could move warm water noiselessly through baseboard convectors, or electric fans could force warmed air to every corner of a building. In addition, these motors could be controlled with electric signals from thermostats so that a steady temperature could be automatically maintained.

By the early part of this century the technology of heating with mechanical systems had been worked out fairly well. But heating is only one-half of the climatic control problem and by far the easier to solve. It is much simpler to generate and retain heat than to dispose of it. In hot, dry climates people have long taken advantage of evaporation as a way to cool the air. Systems of fountains, plants, and even permeable clay pots filled with water were used to both cool and humidify the air. But in humid climates, evaporation is greatly inhibited and radiational cooling to the night sky is also reduced. This made it nearly impossible to cool a place in hot, humid weather until the advent of air-conditioning technology.

Willis Carrier, the father of air conditioning, began this revolution when he hit upon a way to both dehumidify and cool air. He developed the rather paradoxical system of dehumidifying air by passing it through a spray of water. It was based on the principle that cold air cannot hold as much absolute humidity as warm air. By passing warm humid air through a spray of chilled water, the air was cooled and thus forced to lose its excess humidity, which would then condense out onto the surface of the water droplets in the spray. By choosing how cold the water spray was, Carrier could also choose exactly how much humidity would be left in the air. He would then reheat the air to a comfortable room temperature and have air at precisely the temperature and relative humidity that he desired. With Carrier's discovery, for the first time all the elements of thermal control were available.

Once the technology was developed to control completely the thermal environment, people became curious about what a truly optimal thermal environment might be. A great deal of research has since been done to determine the effects of temperature on human beings, and to pinpoint the "comfort zone" where a person functions most efficiently. It has been found that people are surprisingly sensitive to subtle changes in temperature. Givoni describes experiments that test the sensitivity to still-air temperature using a scale from 0 to 9. These experiments have shown that a person can consistently distinguish not only between such levels as warm versus slightly warm but even such small differences as 4.2 (not entirely comfortable, but definitely not slightly warm) or 4.7 (less than slightly warm, but definitely not comfortable). While every person has his or her own scale, each individual is remarkably consistent.[5] Similarly, studies have shown that people can sense very small gradations in the radiant temperature. In one experiment subjects were put in the center of a room with constant air temperature, but where the surface temperatures of the end walls could be regulated. A majority of the subjects could notice a 5°C elevation in the temperature of one of the walls, a miniscule change in the average radiant temperature.[6]

This sensitivity of perception, however, does not preclude people from maintaining comfort through a wide range of thermal conditions. Studies of the "comfort zone," or zone of thermal neutrality, for lightly clothed, sedentary individuals show considerable variation. According to one report, the British comfort zone lies between 58°F and 70°F, the comfort zone in the United States lies between 69° and 80°; and in the tropics it is between 74° and 85°.[7] A comfort zone also varies enormously with each individual and according to such factors as age, sex, and acclimatization. Without standardized light clothing and low activity levels, one can assume that the range of thermal conditions within which a person can be comfortable is far greater.

Despite this variation, the notion of a thermal optimum persists. The American Society of Heating, Refrigeration, and Air-conditioning Engineers (ASHRAE) has published standards for thermal comfort that are used across the country and have been incorporated into many municipal and state building codes. There is an underlying assumption that the best thermal environment never needs to be noticed and that once an objectively "comfortable" thermal environment has been provided, all of our thermal needs will have been met. The use of all of our extremely sophisticated environmental control systems is directed to this one end—to produce standard comfort zone conditions.

A parallel might be drawn to the provision of our nutritional needs. Food is as basic to our survival as is our thermal environment. Just as thermal needs have been studied, so scientists have also studied the basic nutritional requirements of human beings. Our level of understanding makes it theoretically possible to provide for all of our nutritional needs with a few pills and injections. However, while eating is a basic physiological necessity, no one would overlook the fact that it also plays a profound role in the cultural life of a people. A few tubes of an astronaut's nutritious goop are no substitute for a gourmet meal. They lack sensuality—taste, aroma, texture, temperature, color. They are disconnected from all the customs that have developed around eating—the specific types of food and social setting associated with breakfast, with a family dinner, with a sweet treat. And they have none of the potential for significance of those special foods used for ceremonial occasions such as a birthday cake, the Thanksgiving turkey, the symbolic foods of a Seder.

The thermal environment also has the potential for such sensuality, cultural roles, and symbolism that need not, indeed should not, be designed out of existence in the name of a thermally neutral world.

Delight

People have a sense of warmth and coolness, a thermal sense like sight or smell, although it is not normally counted in the traditional list of our five senses. It is usually included with other aspects of the sense of touch. They are taken as one, probably because the thermal sense is located in our skin where our senses of touch and pressure also lie, or perhaps because we notice the temperature of something most accurately when we touch it directly, that is, when we conduct heat to or from it. But the thermal sense is definitely a separate sense, for we have specialized nerve endings whose only function is to tell us if some part of our body is getting cooler or warmer.

As with all our other senses, there seems to be a simple pleasure that comes with just using it, letting it provide us with bits of information about the world around, using it to explore and learn, or just to notice. The stone is cool; yes, it feels cool when I touch it; perhaps it has been in the shade for a while. The coffee cup is warm; it warms my hands. There is something very affirming of one's own life in being aware of these little pieces of information about the world outside us. When the sun is warm on my face and the breeze is cool, I know it is good to be alive.

There is a basic difference, however, between our thermal sense and all of our other senses. When our thermal sensors tell us an object is cold, that object is already making us colder. If, on the other hand, I look at a red object it won't make me grow redder, nor will touching a bumpy object make me bumpy. Thermal information is never neutral; it always reflects what is directly happening to the body. This is because the thermal nerve endings are heat-flow sensors, not temperature sensors. They can't tell directly what the temperature of something is; rather, they monitor how quickly our bodies are losing or gaining heat. From this information we judge how much colder or warmer than body temperature an object is. For example, if I touch a piece of wood and a piece of metal that are both at room temperature, the metal will feel colder because it absorbs the heat from my hand more quickly.

As long as the temperature differential isn't very great, our bodies can use one of their metabolic strategies to adapt to the new conditions and the thermal stimulus will no longer be noticeable. Thus, when I walk into a warm room, I notice at once how warm the air is. Within a few minutes, however, I have adjusted and the room feels normal. Or rather, I feel normal in the room. We might draw a parallel with the fatigue experienced by the other senses (although the mechanism is not the same). We can only smell a rose for so long before the smell fades away. The sensors become saturated and attention moves on to new information. Our nervous system is much more attuned to noticing change in the environment than to noticing steady states.

A proper gourmet meal has a wide variety of tastes—salty, sweet, spicy, savory—so that the taste buds can be renewed and experience each flavor afresh. This renewal mechanism seems to be especially active for the thermal sense when we experience a temperature change within the basic comfort zone. There is an extra delight in the delicious comfort of a balmy spring day as I walk beneath a row of trees and sense the alternating warmth and coolness of sun and shade.

We all love having our world full of colors, every color in the rainbow and then some. Even though studies have shown blue to be the most restful color, I doubt that anyone would put forth an argument for a monochromatic world. And yet a steady-state thermal environment is the prevailing standard for office buildings, schools, and homes across the United States. James Marston Fitch nicely sums up this ideal: "The technology of heating and cooling aims . . . to achieve a thermal 'steady-state' across time and a thermal equilibrium across space." In other words a constant temperature everywhere, at all times. He goes on to note that "Neither of these criteria is easy to achieve since radiant and ambient heat are very unstable forms of energy."[1] Such uniformity is extremely unnatural and therefore requires a great deal of effort, and energy, to maintain. Engineers must use extremely sophisticated methods to ensure that every location within an enormous office tower can be maintained at a constant temperature and humidity.

It is not at all uncommon these days in Houston or Los Angeles to drive an air-conditioned car to an air-conditioned office to work until it is time to go to dinner in an air-conditioned restaurant before seeing a movie in an air-conditioned theater. Of course, there is the brief inconvenience of a blast of hot air between the car and the office. To remedy this, it is occasionally proposed that a large bubble be put over the whole city, perhaps a pneumatic structure or one of Buckminster Fuller's domes. This climatic envelope would enable the entire city to be air conditioned, indoors and outdoors. Indeed, "outdoors" would be a thing of the past. This approach is being considered on a relatively small scale in the plans for a new General Services Administration building in Colorado. A landscape of low rise structures will be contained within a transparent pneumatic bubble. The buildings will need no windows or doors or individual heating plants because the entire landscape will be maintained at the same comfortable temperature.

The steady-state approach to the thermal environment assumes that any degree of thermal stress is undesirable. A constant temperature is maintained in order to save people from the effort and the distraction of adjusting to different conditions. And yet, in spite of the extra physiological effort required to adjust to thermal stimuli, people definitely seem to enjoy a range of temperatures. Indeed, they frequently seek out an extreme thermal environment for recreation or vacations. This must explain in large part the love of the Finns for their saunas and the Japanese for their scalding hot baths. Americans flock to beaches in the summer to bake in the sun and travel great distances in the winter to ski on frosty mountain tops. People relish the very hotness or coldness of these places.

We should note that all of these places of thermal extremes have their opposites close at hand. The Finns make a practice of jumping from the sauna into a snowbank or a cold lake. At the beach, after baking in the hot sun, there is the cold ocean to swim in. The skier freezes on the slope, knowing all the while that the lodge waits down below with a roaring fire and some warming libation. There are probably two reasons for having the extremes right next to each other. The first is physiological: the availability of extremes ensures that we can move from one to the other to maintain a thermal balance. This gives us the safety to enjoy fully both extremes. We can be greatly overheated for a while and then chilled to the bone, all without threatening our health. Indeed, proponents of the sauna claim it even strengthens one's health and improves resistance to cold. H. J. Viherjuuri, a historian of the sauna, quotes an entertaining description by an Italian traveler of the eighteenth century who encountered some Finns after their sauna:

> In winter they often go out completely naked and roll
>
> themselves in the snow, while the temperature is 40

or 50 degrees below zero. They wander naked in the open air, talking to each other and even with a chance passerby. If a traveler in search of help happens to arrive in a remote village at the time when all the inhabitants are in the sauna, they will leave the bathhouse in order to harness or unharness a horse, to fetch hay, or to do anything else without ever thinking of putting any clothes on. Meanwhile the traveler, although enveloped in a fur coat, is stiff with cold, and does not dare to take off his gloves. What astonishes the people of our climate most is that no ill effects ensue from this sudden change of temperature. People who live in warmer climates, on the other hand . . . are liable to get rheumatism even when the most gentle wind blows.[2]

The second reason to have thermal extremes close together might be termed aesthetic. The experience of each extreme is made more acute by contrast to the other. We need not even directly experience both extremes in order to savor their contrast. Simply being reminded of the cold winter storm outside can make us enjoy the warmth of the fireside more intensely, as John Greenleaf Whittier so vividly recounts in his poem "Snowbound":

> *Shut in from all the world without,*
>
> *We sat the clean-winged hearth about,*
>
> *Content to let the north-wind roar*

In baffled rage at pane and door,

While the red logs before us beat

The frost-line back with tropic heat;

And ever, when a louder blast

Shook beam and rafter as it passed,

The merrier up its roaring draught

The great throat of the chimney laughed.

Perhaps the desire for contrast is a reason why the gardens of Islam had to be contained by high walls. The garden, with its flowers, shade trees, and fountains provided a cool refuge from the desert heat. The bright sun and hot desert air could not be completely excluded, but the walls sharply defined the limits of the garden and concentrated the sense of its lush coolness. Certainly, the high walls were a way to ensure privacy, so important for the Muslim. But the walls' highly visible presence also served to emphasize the difference between the cool garden within and the hot desert without.

Since our thermal sensors are not distance receptors, that is, they cannot warn us that a place will be cold before it starts to chill our body, we have to rely on other senses to give us advance clues. We look for qualities that have been associated with warmth or coolness in our past experience. Does the place have soft fuzzy surfaces? Perhaps it will be warm like my wool sweater is. Are the colors reds and browns? Then maybe it will be warm like a room lit by the red-gold light of a fire. Are there mellow aromas? Then surely it will be warm like a kitchen full of people and spices and bread baking.

Such clues from other senses can become so strongly associated with a sense of coolness or warmth that they can occasionally substitute for the thermal experience itself. For example, the taste of mint in drink or food seems refreshing and cool regardless of what temperature it is. Similarly, in order to feel warm and cozy at night, many people find that they must have a heavy set of blankets to cover them while they sleep, even though one light fluffy quilt would be a better insulator. The pressure of the blankets conveys a feeling of warmth quite independent of their actual thermal qualities. An example related by Tetsuro Yoshida suggests that the Japanese are masters of the substitution of one sense for another. He reports: "In the summer the householder likes to hang a picture of a waterfall, a mountain stream, or similar view in the Tokonoma and enjoy in its contemplation a feeling of coolness."[3]

One of the magical things about our senses is that they do not function in isolation. Each sense contributes to the fuller comprehension of other sensory information. Indeed, one may not even be able to understand the information from one sense properly until it can be related to information from other senses. For instance, a person blind from birth because of a congenital cataract, who then has sight restored by surgery, must learn to see. At first the field of vision consists of light patterns, flat and meaningless. Gradually specific light patterns are associated with the understanding of the world that was previously developed from the other senses. In order to learn to see three dimensionally, one must touch, rotate, walk around things. By associating sight with bodily movement and touch, the brain begins to perceive form and depth and perspective.

Looking at a photograph of a place, we are limited to purely visual clues about its thermal qualities, yet we still can perceive it to be a warm or a cool place, thermally pleasant or unpleasant. A picture of a mosque in Isfahan, for example, with its polished marble floors and heavy masonry walls, its high airy vaults and deeply shaded recesses, looks invitingly cool and refreshing. Of course, we imagine it to be in the hot desert sun of Iran. With almost the same set of visual clues— heavy masonry, smooth polished surfaces, high airy colonnades—a building in Germany, such as one of the neoclassical government buildings of the twenties and thirties, comes across as forbiddingly cold and inhospitable. Our visual perceptions might mislead us completely. Both places could conceivably be heated by a hidden radiant system. With our current technology the temperature of a place need not be associated with the form of the building or the materials used or the region where it is located. But how unsatisfying is this dissociation of warmth or coolness from all of our other senses!

To enjoy being warmed or cooled we need some awareness of the process. Clearly, it is impossible to enjoy consciously what we don't notice; yet, most of the processes of heat flow take place below our level of conscious sensation. Most of the mechanisms of cooling, for example, are especially subtle. Heat usually convects away from our skin surfaces in air currents too gentle to discern. Similarly most perspiration evaporates before we perceive our skin to be moist. Clues from other senses can help make us more aware of thermal processes, enabling us to derive more enjoyment from them. For instance, there are many ways to notice that the air is moving and helping to cool us even when it is too gentle to feel. Ho Hsun, a Chinese poet, expressed it well:

> You can't see it or hear it,
>
> It is so soft. But it is strong enough
>
> To dust the mirror with pollen,
>
> And thrum the strings of the lute. [4]

Yoshida reports that in the hot and humid Japanese summer "People like to hang a lantern or a wind chime under the roof of the veranda. The lightly swaying lantern or the ringing of the bell gives a suggestion of refreshing wind and coolness."[5] In Persian gardens roses and jasmine and other fragrant flowers were planted in different quarters so that when the breeze came, it came "loaded with scents."

Many of the other sensory associations with cooling seem to want to remind us of something, like the breeze, lightly playing over a surface. Cooling sounds are light and high pitched, like the Japanese wind chimes or the splashing of water droplets in a fountain. Cool decorations move lightly over a surface, like the lattice work and laciness of a Victorian gazebo or the mosaics of vines and script that twine endlessly over every surface of a Persian mosque. Indeed, it is right at the skin's surface that people most consciously notice cooling. This makes perfect sense when we consider that both the processes of evaporation and convection take place at the surface of the skin. Even when losing body heat by radiation to a cold surface, people still assume that they are being chilled by a cold draft somewhere in the room. People also feel chilled, to the point of getting goosebumps, if their skin is lightly touched, as with the brush of a feather, even though there is no temperature change at all.

In contrast, there is something basically internal about warmth, probably because we associate it with the warmth generated within our own bodies. Warmth is what's alive at the very core of things. A fire and the sun also generate heat inside of themselves. We feel their heat not so much warming our skin as penetrating into the very center of our being.

Other than a fire or the sun, we are generally the warmest things in our environment, our own source of heat. Thus, when it is cold out, the best way to get warm is to insulate our bodies: to be surrounded by thick, fluffy clothing; to sink into a deep, overstuffed chair; to huddle inside of a small, close-sheltering building. These are all just big enough to enclose our bodies, preventing heat from dispersing very far. Bodies of other people, and animals, can also be sources of heat. To be close to someone is to share in their warmth, both physically and emotionally. Places that remind us of the presence of people, of the life and activities that they generate, capture some of this sense of warmth. The Victorian parlor, with all of its clutter, its remnants of people's lives, its deep upholstered chairs and layers of rugs and curtains and hangings and pictures, has this sense of warmth. The sounds and smells of people all indicate their presence and, thus, their warmth. Things that were once alive and warm themselves, like the fur of a polar bear rug, or the leather of a chair, perhaps even the sheep's wool in a sweater, may carry an association with that previous life and so seem even warmer.

When we get cold, our muscles tense up, trying to generate more heat, and capillaries at the skin's surface constrict. These physiological responses leave us feeling tense and numb. Places that seem warm offer an antidote to the tension and numbness with things that are comforting and soothing: a soft, flowing light; the deep plush of a velvet chair; or the low, resonant notes of a blues song. They help to relax us in the same way that the warmth of a fire, or even a drink of liquor, penetrates through the body and relaxes the muscles.

When we are overheated we often need the opposite antidote. The heat makes us lethargic and slow-witted. Any action requires too much effort. There is delight, then, to be had in things that provide a little liveliness for us, like the splashing of a fountain or the sparkle and flutter of Japanese street decorations. Their activity helps the mind feel a bit more quick-witted and lively in spite of the dullness of a hot, muggy day. A hot day, however, can also be stressful because it overstimulates. The sun can be too bright, glinting off of every surface, accompanied by an inescapable dry wind that exhausts the nerves. The antidote then is not something that moves and sparkles but a deep, quiet coolness, a place to retreat from the sun and rest in peace. Deeply shaded Islamic prayer halls, with their seemingly endless repetition of columns and arches, produce this calming effect. The classical Persian garden is intended to provide the antidote to both the lethargy and the exhaustion of the senses. There is the liveliness of the fountains and the overhanging vines with their fluttering leaves that create a dappled light. And there are also areas of still water and large stone pavilions that create a deep, quiet shade. One is free to move among these different elements and to choose the place where the balance of liveliness and quietude are just right. The Persian garden offers an amazing richness and variety of sensory experiences which all serve to reinforce the pervasive sense of coolness.

Each sense not only gives us different information about the world but also has its own quality, its own evocations. Yi-Fu Tuan has made some interesting correlations between the senses and one's perception of the world. The sense of smell seems to be somehow linked with our faculties of memory. Tuan writes that "Odor has the power to evoke vivid, emotionally-charged memories of past events and scenes. A whiff of sage may call to mind an entire complex of sensations: the image of great rolling plains covered with grass and specked with clumps of sagebrush, the brightness of the sun, the heat, the bumpiness of the road."[6] Or the same smell of sage, often used in turkey stuffing, might call forth all of the warmth and intimacy of Thanksgiving. Sight is perhaps more difficult to categorize because it functions on so many complex levels. But clearly, it is most important to our spatial understanding of the world. It allows us to see three dimensionally, to judge distance, and thus to understand the relationship of one thing to another. In English, "I see" means "I understand." But vision is also rather static. Although we see motion, we tend to remember visually only a fixed image. Hearing, on the other hand, seems to be strongly associated with a sense of time. A song or a melody to be remembered must be remembered in time. Tuan writes, "With deafness, life seems frozen and time lacks progression."[7] The sense of touch has an immediacy to it. If we can touch something, we are persuaded that it is not an illusion or a hallucination but that it is very real—right here and now—like pinching your-self to see if you are dreaming. The thermal sense cannot be easily isolated from overall experience, unlike seeing or hearing. We cannot close it off, like closing our eyes. Nor does it provide highly differentiated information, as does the individuality of a person's voice, or even smell. The thermal sense is, however, intricately bound up with the experience of our bodies. We continually sense the heat flow of our bodies, information that creates a general background for all other experience.

Since each sense contributes a slightly different perception of the world, the more senses involved in a particular experience, the fuller, the rounder, the experience becomes. If sight allows for a three-dimensional world, then each other sense contributes at least one, if not more, additional dimensions. The most vivid, most powerful experiences are those involving all of the senses at once.

Perhaps the human fascination with fire stems from the totality of its sensory stimulation. The fire gives a flickering and glowing light, ever moving, ever changing. It crackles and hisses and fills the room with the smells of smoke and wood and perhaps even food. It penetrates us with its warmth. Every sense is stimulated and all of their associated modes of perception, such as memory and an awareness of time, are also brought into play, focused on the one experience of the fire. Together they create such an intense feeling of reality, of the "here and nowness" of the moment, that the fire becomes completely captivating. We are likely to feel that we could spend hours mesmerized by it. Indeed, Gaston Bachelard makes an eloquent case that "Reverie before a burning fire is . . . the first and the most truly human use of fire."[8]

Islamic gardens also offer delights for each sense; they seem to have a power similar to that of fire to captivate the imagination. A Turkish garden motto states clearly the provisions for the senses:

> *Roses for perfume,*
>
> *Nightingales for song,*
>
> *And the sight and sound*
>
> > *of running water.*

A sixteenth-century traveler furnished an eyewitness description of the delights of a Persian garden during its golden age:

> The garden I shall describe was constructed in such a way that two courses of crystal-clear water met before a building, forming a large lake in which countless swans, geese and ducks disported themselves. Below this lake were seven waterfalls—as many as there are planets. . . . From the lake jets of water spouted up so high into the air that the spray, as it descended, was like a rain of diamonds. How often was I moved by the rippling of the fountains and the murmuring of the brook as it streamed downhill, over the terraces of the garden, hemmed in by rose bushes, willows, and acacias. I cried with sheer joy until the exceeding beauty and the rushing of the water rocked me to sleep.[9]

Affection

Keeping warm and keeping cool have been everyday activities for people since time immemorial. But they proceed at an almost unconscious level of culture, for these actions are so common and usually so well integrated with all the other aspects of the culture that people don't often notice their particular character as a response to thermal need. It is only the rare literary traveler who may remark how a peoples' customs are suited to the local climate—a subject for travel essays only slightly more sophisticated than remarking on the weather itself. And yet from the minute scale of gesture and posture to the grand scale of ritual and festivals, social customs often involve a thermal aspect. The image of a Southern lady nervously fanning herself is that of a coquette using the fan as a prop for flirting, rather than a woman merely trying to cool herself. Europeans have the custom of using furniture, chairs and beds, to raise themselves conveniently above the cold air that accumulates at floor level. Hindus, on the other hand, use no such furniture but sit directly on the floor where they benefit from the extra coolness held in the ground. Christmas is known as a religious festival. Yet the notion of celebrating Christmas in the southern hemisphere at the height of midsummer heat is slightly unsettling to people in the northern hemisphere. In spite of its religious basis, Christmas has strong connotations of being a warm, cozy time set in contrast to midwinter cold. Similarly every culture has its set of rituals, customs, and special activities associated with each season.

In agricultural communities the world over life has always changed radically with the seasons. Not only were different crops cared for but other jobs, rituals, clothes, and festivals were all associated with the particular weather and thermal conditions of each season. John F. Embree, in his study *Suye Mura: A Japanese Village*, presents a chart that details how all of the jobs done in the village have a special seasonal time slot. He explains,

> In addition to the seasonal nature of sowing and harvesting the crops, there is a set season for making most of the village's products. A year's supply of hair oil is pressed in spring before the work of wheat harvest and rice planting begins. . . . Each season has its characteristic clothing, even the games children play are seasonal—girls bounce balls in fall and juggle bean bags in the spring; boys chase dragon flies and walk on stilts in the summer. . . . The only aspect of life in the [village] not directly or indirectly affected by the seasons are those works of fate—birth and death.[1]

Obviously, much of this was determined more by the cycles of plant and animal growth than directly by temperature, but the thermal conditions that coincide with these cycles are inextricably associated with the activities and rituals and serve to reinforce their importance.

In the same way that customs can come to be associated with seasonal and thermal qualities, many seemingly mundane objects in our lives can also come to have strong thermal associations. Tea pots are warm things because they hold hot tea. Yet even when they are empty they have a sense of warmth that lingers about them. The toddler who drags his security blanket everywhere may love it most as a reminder of the sense of warmth and well-being it gives him in his bed, not so different from the security and warmth of being held by his mother. Like the toddler, we tend to cherish the things that have provided us with warmth or coolness just when we needed or wanted it. This association between an object and our thermal well-being may become semiconscious and vague, and yet it can strongly contribute to our affection for the object. How hard it is to give up the old misshapen sweater or the old shade hat that kept the sun off for so long. They are rather like old friends who have done us a good turn over and over again.

Places are especially likely to have thermal associations, for the provision of shelter, or the creation of a favorable microclimate, is one of the most basic functions of building. A place with strong thermal associations may be an everyday sort of place, like a breakfast room where the sun streams in each morning, or it may be somewhere we go only for special occasions, like a shady park pavilion for summer picnics. It might even be a place we have never experienced directly but that we can fantasize about as having wonderful thermal qualities. A mountain cabin deep in the winter snow can convey a sense of cozy shelter even when it is just an image in a photograph.

The fondness many Americans have for the four-poster bed may be simply because it is a nostalgic reminder of the colonial era, like turned maple furniture or an eagle over the front door. Yet there is probably also an awareness that it provided a cozy retreat where one was assured of finding warmth and comfort. With its canopy, and curtains that could be drawn to prevent drafts and retain body-warmed air, the four-poster bed was a snug enclave within the cold and drafty old houses.

The inglenook, the gazebo, and the porch swing are other examples of places with special thermal functions. The inglenook,

33

often more of a small room enclosing the fireplace than a nook, was an old medieval English device which was revived at the turn of the century by Frank Lloyd Wright, C. F. A. Voysey, and their contemporaries. Like the four-poster bed, an inglenook creates the image of a special warm enclave, for its function is intuitively clear: with seats built in along the walls, it is just large enough for a few people to gather close to the fire's radiant warmth and be shielded from drafts.

The airy Victorian gazebo was perhaps the thermal antithesis of the inglenook. With an open structure and a light, umbrella-like roof, the gazebo was set out on an open lawn where it could provide a bit of shade while catching every passing breeze. Usually painted white, with lacy Victorian scroll-work, the gazebo designated a certain spot as the cool and shady place to be on a hot summer's day.

The American porch swing is another interesting example. The creaking, wood-slatted swing out on the front porch may now be something of a cliché as a setting for courtship in the South, but until the availability of air conditioning, it was a thermal necessity. The swing was a most effective way to get a bit of cooling ventilation to relieve the heat in the still, sultry nights of the American South. In place of fanning oneself, the gentle swinging moved air past the entire body with very little effort expended. It is little wonder that such a pleasant system of cooling provided a favorite place for visiting and courting.

The inglenook and the gazebo may seem more like settings for a children's story than examples of thermal environments relevant to today's needs. Yet the very affection with which they are remembered, revealed in the bits of romance or nostalgia attached to them, suggests that there is something of value to be learned from them. The words we use to describe such places—snug and cozy or airy and refreshing—all imply that these places offer us a sense of thermal well-being. And it is partly this association of the experience of well-being with a particular place that leads us to think of it fondly. As with the toddler's blanket or the old sun hat, we can develop an emotional attachment to the places that have been responsible for pleasant moments in our lives.

Fondness for a particular place or thing is often manifested in the extra care that people invest in it, especially in decoration. The elaborate and colorful patterns of a patchwork quilt suggest that it is well loved by someone. The decorative designs often embossed on a woodburning stove indicate it is not regarded merely as a functional appliance but as a special object deserving of a little extra attention. Similarly, the choice of the mantel as the place for precious objects a family wants to display bespeaks the importance of the hearth in the family's life.

We need an object for our affections, something identifiable on which to focus attention. If there is something very individual and particular that we consider responsible for our well-being—a stove that is the source of all warmth, for example—we can focus appreciation for our comfort on that one thing. But if nothing seems to be responsible for our sense of well-being, then what or whom do we thank? On a lovely spring day we may identify the season itself with our wonderful sense of well-being, as has been done in hundreds of songs about the joys of spring. On a tropical isle that has an ever-perfect combination of balmy breezes, warming sunshine, and shady palms, we would probably come to love the island for providing us with such a fortuitous setting. But in a typical office building, to what can we attribute the all-pervasive comfort of 70°F, 50 per cent relative humidity? The air diffuser hidden in the hung ceiling panels? The maintenance personnel who work during off-hours? The mechanical equipment down in the basement below the parking garage? The engineer who designed the system long ago? The whole vast building itself? Most likely, we would simply take it all for granted. When thermal comfort is a constant condition, constant in both space and time, it becomes so abstract that it loses its potential to focus affection.

We are also unlikely to relate our thermal well-being to anything in particular unless there is an awareness at some level that an object or place does indeed have a thermal function. Radiant hot-water pipes embedded in a ceiling may do an admirable job of keeping us warm and comfortable, but there is no way to sense directly that the ceiling has a thermal function. The radiant level is generally far too gentle to notice, nor is there any way to see or hear or feel that the ceiling is "on." The lack of specific clues makes it hard to relate to the ceiling in the same way we relate to, say, the hearth.

The same can be said of walls. An important function of the exterior wall of a building, especially in a cold climate, is to act as an insulator between the interior of the building and the weather conditions outside. To improve the thermal performance of modern light-weight construction, we stuff the wall with a thick blanket of fiberglass fuzz. The insulation is then completely covered over with finish materials so that only someone who had built the wall would be aware of its anatomy and thus be able to fully appreciate it for its thermal abilities.

Compare this to a highly visible system of insulation from the Middle Ages—the use of exquisite, intricately woven tapestries and carpets in the great medieval halls. The practice originated with the European peasants who would hang skins or lengths of cloth on the walls of their houses during the cold weather. This created an extra insulating air space and a radiation barrier between the inhabitants and the cold exterior walls. Eventually royalty took to commissioning the weaving of very special pictorial hangings, the tapestries, to grace the ever-cold stone walls of their castles. Such tapestries clearly transcended their role as insulators and evolved into one of the high art forms of the period.

The Mughuls of India developed a similar system in order to heat their open and airy stone palaces in winter. Collections of Persian carpets, in addition to providing insulating layers over the stone floors for people to sit on, were also hung from hooks along the walls. Sometimes hung two thick, the carpets created an insulating tent within the room whose richness was certainly fit for a sultan. The carpets were greatly valued for their beauty but also for the sense of warmth and comfort they conveyed. Their removal when the warm weather arrived reinforced their seasonal and thermal associations.

One factor that can help us to appreciate the thermal function of a place or object is variability. We are more likely to notice the function of something if there are times when it is not in operation, to notice the significance of something's presence if there are times when it is not there. Shutters provide an interesting example. Outside window shutters have long been common all over Europe and were a standard feature of buildings in early America. Their function, clearly, is to close off the window to shelter the interior of the house from storm winds or excess heat. Most of the time, however, they are hinged open, hanging at the sides of the windows. Even while open, their presence conveys a reassuring sense of shelter, for there is the implication that they can be closed when needed. This sense of shelter is still evoked by shutters that are only decorative, like the hopelessly narrow ones that frame modern picture windows on houses all over the United States. For many people, a house simply does not look friendly or comfortable without shutters framing its windows. In contrast, the wall of a house has many of the same functions as a shutter—to keep out storm winds or excess heat—and yet we are unlikely to appreciate a wall for those particular functions because it does not go through any changes that would draw our attention to its performance.

Related to shutters are the various systems of movable insulation that are being developed in conjunction with solar design. They would seem to have a similar potential for becoming objects of people's affections. Their relation to thermal function is quite obvious because they are only in place when extra insulation is needed. Many rather friendly systems are being developed. One example is a rolldown shade padded with either quilting or a thin sheet of foam rubber. It is covered with a decorative fabric and is held snug against the inside of a window frame to prevent drafts. Pulling down these shades becomes a bit like putting the house to bed at night. Another example is an insulating louver system, developed by Zomeworks Corporation, called "Skylid®." The louvers automatically open to let solar radiation in when the sun shines and close in the evening to prevent radiant heat loss. They are ingeniously controlled and driven by the shifting weight of freon, which alternately vaporizes and condenses to shift the balance of the louvers. A couple who have installed some Skylids in their house to assist in solar collection describe how the louvers have heightened their awareness of thermal processes: "We look into the greenhouse and watch the Skylids closing automatically, one by one and in no particular order, and we are aware of hot air rising, cold air settling. . . . [They] remind us that the earth is turning and the day is ending."[2]

The most direct experience of a thermal process is through conduction, for the sense of touch has an immediacy and undeniable reality to it. Whenever we touch something, we automatically receive information about its temperature whether or not we consciously take note. Our affection for many everyday objects may be derived partly from simply enjoying their warmth or coolness as we touch them. An Englishman's fondness for his pipe may come in part from cradling its warm bowl in his hand. A pet cat provides a warm body to stroke and creates a pool of warmth as it curls contentedly in one's lap. (Don't be flattered, she is just after *your* warmth.)

Conduction can also play a role in our relationship to the larger environment. The most commonly experienced conductive environment is water. When we immerse ourselves in water, its temperature is always an important consideration because we exchange heat with it so quickly. People are very careful about how cold their cold bath really is. They have a wide range of descriptions for water temperature, from tepid and lukewarm to scalding. In northern China and Korea there is a raised earthen platform inside the house called a k'ang. Heated by the flues from the kitchen stove that are buried within, it provides a warm surface on which to sit. It is on the k'ang that the family sits to eat meals, to do household chores, and to spend its leisure time in talking and telling stories. Sand dunes in Saudi Arabia are another interesting example of a conductive environment. In the villages people commonly go out in the evening to sit and talk on a nearby sand dune. On a hot night the north slope of a dune offers a very comfortable and cooling place to sit. When the nights get cooler, people choose instead to sit against the slope that is still warm from the late-afternoon sun.

On the whole, though, conductive environments are rather rare. Instead of through the immediacy of conduction, our thermal relationship with a place is more likely to be established through convection, evaporation, and radiant exchange. We may note these processes in the extreme cases: the very hot air of the sauna is unforgettable, and the radiant heat from a very hot source such as a stove, a fire, or the sun, is certainly noticeable. But more often these processes operate below our consciously sensible level. We may still perceive a place to be warm and comfortable, or cool and relaxing, but without necessarily noting exactly why or how. The thermal information is not differentiated in our memory; rather, it is retained as a quality, or underlying tone, associated with the whole experience of the place. It contributes to our sense of the particular personality, or spirit, that we identify with that place. In remembering the spirit of a place, we can anticipate that if we return, we will have the same sense of comfort or relaxation as before.

The four-poster bed provides a good example of a place that is not warm in itself yet carries strong thermal associations. It slowly becomes warm as the air within the drawn curtains is warmed by body heat. While such a thermal process is a bit subtle to perceive, the overall experience of warmth can be related to the context of a very distinct and identifiable place. The limits of the space are clearly marked by the four posts that frame the bed. The space is further enclosed by the curtains hung from the frame. Such strong spatial definition ensures that our memories will associate the experience of thermal comfort with something in particular—the place itself.

The inglenook, the gazebo, and the porch swing also have strong definitions of their spaces. They are each a bit like a little house set off for a special thermal purpose. They might be termed "thermal aediculae." Although the term aedicula is most often used in conjunction with a sacred or ceremonial little house, it can also be used to describe any diminutive structure used to mark a place as special. Summerson, in his wonderful essay on the use of the aedicula in Gothic architecture, relates it to the urge of the child to hide under a chair or table and pretend that he is in his own house. Summerson contends that there is a basic human "fascination of the miniature shelter."[3] Perhaps this is because the aedicula intensifies one's experience of the place by working somewhat like a caricature. By reducing some things in scale, it exaggerates the importance of other things, most especially the size of a person in relation to the space. Making thermal places that incorporate the qualities of an aedicula is a way to emphasize the importance of the place as a setting for people.

Special little thermal places like the inglenook or gazebo now seem rather quaint and old-fashioned because they have been outmoded by a technology that enables us to keep whole buildings at a uniform temperature. We no longer need to create the one special place that will have just the right thermal qualities, for every place can now be just right. Yet the lingering fondness we have for such places suggests they served some need especially well. Each one provided a setting for the activities associated with a specific set of thermal conditions. People's daily habits and spatial patterns were in large part determined by the availability of desirable thermal qualities. In southern Italy women often do their sewing sitting in the open doorways of their houses where they can make subtle adjustments in the position of their chairs according to how much sunlight or shade, warmth from the sun or coolness from the house interior, they desire.

In America our tendency has been to get away from thermal conditions as a determinant of behavior. Instead, we have used our technology to keep entire living and working complexes at a uniformly comfortable temperature. As a result, our spatial habits have become diffused, and activities that were once localized by thermal conditions have spread out over a whole house or building. We forget, unless the system breaks down, that such wide-ranging use of space is extremely dependent upon the available heating and cooling equipment.

Lawrence Wylie, a Harvard anthropologist, tellingly describes how his family had to readjust their entire domestic pattern when they left their modern American home, "where a movement of a finger regulates the heat of the whole house," to live in a French village. He writes,

> There were fireplaces in every room; there was the
> kitchen stove; there was a salamander—a kind of

Franklin stove—in my study. I was determined to keep the house warm, since with all this apparatus it was theoretically possible. For a few days I went from stove to fireplace to salamander to furnace, nourishing the various fires with wood and coal briquets. It did not take me long to discover that it was a full-time job to keep all these fires burning. . . . Even by spending time and money to heat the house, I was not accomplishing my purpose. When the mistral blew, no fire could keep my study warm. I gave up heating it and brought my typewriter and books and papers into the salle. Then it seemed foolish to have fires going in the fireplaces in the bedrooms when the only times they were useful were when we were dressing and undressing. It was more sensible to dress and undress in the salle. The bathroom was no longer a comfortable refuge as it was at home. . . . We found that we needed fewer baths than before. . . . When one of the children had an earache at night we could not sit in his room and rock him; we brought him down and held him on our lap in front of the fire. The fire of oak logs which burned day and night for six months became the focal point of our family life.

Their spatial behavior, indeed all of their behavior, changed in response to the new (old) heating system:

> Little by little, our family life, which at home was distributed throughout the entire house and which we had tried to distribute throughout the Peyrane house, withdrew from all other rooms and was concentrated in the *salle*. . . . I had to learn to work while the children were playing. The children had to learn to play more quietly. I had to learn to pick up my paper from the table so that it might be used as a dining-room table. . . . Without realizing it we had adapted ourselves to a necessary condition of life in Peyrane where families learn to live together in one room. . . . It is inevitable that the English word "home" cannot be translated directly into French. The nearest equivalent in French is the word *foyer*, the hearth.[4]

There were also seasonal patterns in the use of space that the family found significant: "In the summer this center of life is less important. The fire is lighted only to cook the food. The family lives outdoors in the sun as much as possible."[5] Thus in the summer social life becomes much more public, moving out into the village streets and plazas, to open-air cafes and boule courts, where either warming sun or cooling shade could be found, as necessary.

The great fondness of Mediterranean cultures for their streets and plazas is largely thermal. A great deal of social life goes on in the streets and plazas because they offer the greatest thermal comfort.

They provide a place to bask in the sun or a shady and airy place to be cool, while the houses are stuffy and either too cool from the night before or overheated by the afternoon sun. In most Mediterranean countries the custom of an evening promenade, or *paseo*, developed to take full advantage of the pleasant coolness of the streets and square in the summer's evenings. After the sun has set and the heat of the day is broken, people emerge from their houses and their work —groups of young men or young women, old people with their grandchildren, whole families together—and take a stroll along the *via* and the *piazza* to see whom they may see, to stop and talk, but most simply to enjoy the pleasant air.

Places with desirable thermal qualities naturally tend to become social spaces as people gather to take advantage of the comfort found there. Examples of places with important thermal qualities that are also social spaces abound in every culture. In Saudi Arabia, mosques are designed with a special basement prayer hall that stays cool during the hottest Arabian days. In addition to being used for prayers, it is also a favorite place for the men to stay and socialize or take their afternoon nap. For the women of southern Italy the baker's shop is the place to gather for gossip in the winter, for the ovens make it the warmest place in town. In nineteenth-century America each farmstead or town was likely to have an ice house to store the ice harvested from a pond in winter for use during the summer. The ice house was a much favored, though often illicit, place for children to play during hot weather.

With the advent of air conditioning, businessmen in the United States discovered that coolness could be used to attract the public. The movie house was often the very first place in a small town to be air conditioned. Marquees proclaimed it to be COOL INSIDE. And often some of the chilled air was intentionally spilled out onto the sidewalk to entice the passers-by to come in. In the hot summer months advertisements for modern enclosed shopping malls are sure to mention that the entire complex is air conditioned. It is hoped that people will go there simply to be cool and to see other people, in an American version of the *paseo*—a thermally attracted public which might then be encouraged to buy something.

However, thermal comfort does not just draw people together, it is also an experience to be shared. It is a simple bodily pleasure and, like other basic human experiences such as eating, it is pleasant to share it with people we like. Feeling good together, and being aware of it, creates a certain social bond. It is as simple as, "Yes, we have felt happy and alive together. It is pleasant to be together. We are friends." Thus, sharing a pleasant thermal experience might be a way to reinforce friendship. In northern Indian villages people live with a minimum of furniture, using a simple woven cot, a *charpoy*, as a portable bed, chair, and table all in one. But there is often one very special piece of furniture, occasionally even embellished with decorative carving or painted designs. It is the swing, an indoor swing wide enough for two or three people to sit together. When friends come to visit, the swing is the place to sit for passing the time in easy and intimate socializing. It is the social center, the parlor, of the one-room house.

Sharing the experience of a pleasant thermal setting may also add an extra bonus to courtship. The gentle and cooling breeze of the southern porch swing provided a happy excuse for a couple to sit quietly together. A more technological version might be seen in the type of car that the teenagers of the 1950s considered ideal for a hot date—the convertible. The sheer enjoyment of the cool wind whipping by could put a date in the right mood. Slightly more erotic, perhaps, were the atrium and green houses that were favorite settings for romance in Victorian England. The lovers could get lost among the leaves of the exotic tropical plants and possibly mistake the hot, humid atmosphere for their own concealed passion.

In many cultures a thermal place plays an important role as a setting identified with the cohesion of the family, the clan, or some other social group. The special thermal conditions provide a reason for the group to come together. As with the Wylie family in the French village, economic necessity may enforce a thermal focus of family life in order to conserve effort and resources that must be expended to create extra warmth or coolness. Regardless of the incentive, however, a thermal place provides a particularly appropriate setting to affirm a group's unity, for the individual's enjoyment of the physical comfort reflects on the sense of well-being of the group as a whole.

The hearth is well known to us as the center of family life for European peoples. The Chinese *k'ang* performs a similar function in China and Korea. In Arab villages the coffee pot, with its small fire underneath, forms the focus of the *mudhif,* the social hall, where each evening the village men gather to talk over the day's events. In India the center of the village is traditionally the great shade tree, where the village council meets and where the children are taught to recite the ancient texts.

In Los Angeles the hearth was inherited from European culture as the symbolic center of the home, and almost every house is bound to have a vestigial hearth, whether or not a fire can actually burn there. Yet in the hot climate and affluent economy of Los Angeles, the swimming pool is more likely to be the real focal point of the house. The pool is the place for the family to relax together, floating in its cool waters or simply sitting around its edge. The pool deck provides the setting for family barbecues, birthday parties, and cocktail parties. A typical house plan focuses the view from all the social spaces of the house out onto the pool, the family's pride. Even when inside, an expanse of sliding glass doors allows one to feel intimately associated with the pool's glimmering water.

In Japan the portable *kotatsu* forms something of a focus for family life. The Japanese have notoriously unheatable houses. They have traditionally preferred to design their houses to be cool and airy in summer and then to get by in the winter with localized ways to heat the body. Smallest of all means is the *kairo*, a little case carried around in pockets or between layers of clothes that contains a warm charcoal ember. The *habachi* is a small pot of charcoal that is carried around from room to room to warm the hands. The *kotatsu* is a foot heater that can be shared by a number of feet. It has a low tablelike frame with a quilt over it that is drawn around the body to keep the heat in. Noriko Nishizawa, an architect in Japan, described the role of the *kotatsu* in modern Japanese life: "One can imagine a scene [around the *kotatsu*] like this: children watching TV and/or doing homework, mother knitting or doing some other things. Father . . . may be reading or just lying around. However, today most of the houses have a gas, oil, or electric heater for each room . . . and the families seem to gather less in one room, which is too bad."[6]

Perhaps more important as a social center for the Japanese are the hot baths, which have been called "la grande passion of the Japanese."[7] Ruth Benedict wrote in her study of postwar Japan: "For the poorest rice farmer and the meanest servant, just as for the rich aristocrat, the daily soak in superlatively heated water is part of the routine of every late afternoon."[8] Every village and every neighborhood in a city traditionally has its own communal hot baths where the residents come to bathe together every night. Not to go to the baths means one is sick or angry or antisocial. It is a social occasion, a time to relax after the day's work and enjoy one another's company.

One washes thoroughly before entering the bath so as not to dirty the water for the others. The extremely hot water and steamy atmosphere make one feel almost liquid inside, an inner heat that lasts long after the bath is ended. Villagers used to have no compunction about walking home naked from the bath, for what is the use of clothes when one is warm already? The lingering heat from the bath can also provide partial remedy for the coolness of the Japanese houses. Noriko reports that before she bought a modern heater for her apartment, "I would go to a bath and then go to bed immediately after that in order to keep the heat."[9]

The importance of the social function of the bath has been described by John Embree in his study of a southern Japanese village before the war. Although each household had its own bathhouse, with a tub just big enough for one person, the bath was still a community occasion. Women of neighboring houses took turns doing the work of filling the tub and heating the water, while the others came to use it.

> The evening bath plays an important role in the household life, especially of the women. After the menfolk have bathed, the women will take their turn. If a woman has . . . one or two younger children, they all sit in the tub together. This intimate association every evening creates a strong social bond within the family between the mother and her children. . . . Frequently, two or more women will bathe together, one being in the tub at a time, the others standing by and talking. There is a warm intimacy about these evening chats which keeps close the relationship between the women of three or four neighboring houses. . . .[10]

Noriko reports that although many families today have their own private baths, they will still go to the local public bath "because it is larger and nicer." "Public baths are still popular today and . . . it is a great gathering place for the community. I see old ladies taking ages to put on their clothes because they are too busy gossiping. I am sure the lady in charge of the bath in our town has known all the kids in town since the time they were babies."[11]

A similar social ritual is developing in the apartment complexes and mobile-home parks of California around the Jacuzzi baths. The Jacuzzi provides a place for groups of friends from the complex to get together for a casual visit while they relax in the hot, swirling water. Beginning in the evening, small groups make their way down to the Jacuzzi, knocking on doors to gather friends as they go. Each group has a certain time when it has command of the baths. One group goes before dinner, another right before bed, still another incorporates the time into the traditional cocktail hour and brings drinks.

The association of comfort with people and place are reinforced by the ritualized use of a place. Using a place at a set time and in a specific manner, as the Japanese use their baths, creates a constancy as dependable as the place itself. It establishes, in time and behavior, a definition of the place as strong as any architectural spatial definition, such as an aedicula, might be. Ritualized use can do more than reinforce the affection for a place. Through ritual, a place becomes an essential element in the customs of a people.

Sacredness

Fireplaces have a more significant position in the American home than a simple analysis of their function would indicate. People love having a fireplace, even if they rarely use it. The ostensible function of the fireplace, to provide a source of heat for the house, has long been taken over by far more efficient central heating systems. When a fire is lit, it is likely to be a ceremonial event: a way to make the house feel especially homey, a treat when guests come to visit, a way to give an added air of celebration to a holiday such as Christmas or New Year's. Many modern houses have fireplaces installed with jets of gas that flicker about a permanent concrete log, intended to give the sense of a hearth without the fuss of having to actually build a fire. In such cases it is clear that the fireplace is valued more for its symbolic role than for its thermal function. The meaning the fireplace holds is an extremely important element of what it is. Thus, the hearth is as much a symbolic center of the home as it is a place for burning wood.

There are many other thermal settings in addition to the fireplace that have remarkable significance within their cultures. They are apt to have many layers of meaning, from the most personal, distilled from an individual's unique set of experiences, to those inherited from the experience of a culture as a whole. Yi-Fu Tuan in *Topophilia*, his study of how and why people develop a "love of place," writes that "A symbol is a repository of meanings. Meanings arise out of the more profound experiences that have accumulated through time."[1] To the extent that a place becomes a repository of meanings valued by a culture, it also acquires value by its association with those meanings. In the same way that one can come to love a book because it contains important ideas, so, too, one may value an object or place for the ideas it embodies. In a sense, the place in its role as a symbol stores the idea, giving it a physical reality outside the mind.

In religious societies sacredness is a way to communicate the extreme importance of a symbol to society. When a symbol represents something considered essential to human experience, its preservation is of paramount importance. By deeming it sacred, a symbol becomes inviolable, ensuring its survival through time. The sacredness of the domestic hearth is common to many cultures. Our own concept of the primacy of the hearth may include the image of a fire burning brightly in the parlor of a nineteenth-century family or perhaps stretch back a century or two earlier to the huge central fireplaces of early New England houses. The meanings attached to the hearth, however, have accumulated through a much longer history. They are reflected in traditions having ancient, perhaps prehistoric, roots.

The hearth developed especially great significance in Europe, where pagan religions formed a foundation of ongoing folk traditions long after the establishment of Christianity. Many of the traditions probably grew out of early fire worship rites. It is clear that fire gods were prominent in the pantheons of the Indo-European peoples. The Aryans of Vedic India worshipped the fire god Agni. "He was man's domestic friend, the father of the sacrifice, the mediator between men and gods, the bearer of hymns and prayers from every family altar upwards towards heaven."[2] At the other end of the continent the Irish Celts worshipped Bel, or Baal, to whom they lit great bonfires each May Day, also known as Beltane Eve. James Frazer argues that the great fire festivals of Europe were linked to the annual death and resurrection of the sun: "From the standpoint of primitive man nothing might seem more appropriate than to kindle fires on earth at the two moments when the fire and heat of the great luminary in heaven begins to wane or to wax."[3] Indeed, the solstices, and for some tribes, the equinoxes, were occasions for building huge ceremonial fires, such as the great bonfires burned on Midsummer's Eve in villages all over Europe up through the nineteenth century (and still continuing in Scandinavia). Yuletide, which has come to mean the Christmas season, was originally the name for the heathen winter solstice fire festival. The English custom of the Yule log, which is burned for the Christmas Eve fire, often from a charred fragment saved from the last year's Yule fire, is a remnant of the pagan fire ceremony that has been absorbed into the Christian customs. Frazer explains:

> Certain it is that the winter solstice, which the ancients erroneously assigned to the twenty-fifth of December, was celebrated in antiquity as the Birthday of the Sun, and that festal lights or fires were kindled on this joyful occasion. Our Christmas festival is nothing but a continuation under a Christian name of this old solar festivity; for the ecclesiastical authorities saw fit, about the end of the third or the beginning of the fourth century, arbitrarily to transfer the nativity of Christ from the sixth of January to the twenty-fifth of December, for the purpose of diverting to the Lord the worship which the heathen had hitherto paid on that day to the sun.[4]

The hearth was commonly considered the domestic sanctuary of a fire god. It might have housed a major god who was accepted throughout a whole culture, as in the case of the Agni of the Vedic Hindus, or a small local spirit who was responsible only for the protection of the individual house and its residents. In English folklore there is the tradition of the wise cricket who lives in the hearth and brings good luck and protection to the family. The notion may have originated with the chirping of a real cricket taking up residence in the recesses of the fireplace, but it also seems to have become a diminutive version of the ancient fire spirit who lived in the hearth. Much of the content of these traditions has long ago been abandoned or forgotten; yet they have left a sort of emotional residue, or a vague cultural memory, that continues to contribute to the cultural significance of the hearth.

The sauna presents an example rather closely related to the hearth. In Finland it has a very important place in national custom. The present-day rituals surrounding the sauna are similar to those of the Japanese bath. Although the Finns usually go to the sauna only once a week, in contrast to the daily visits of the Japanese, the sauna remains important as the place and the time for the family to relax together. H. J. Viherjuuri writes, "Reference to the sauna found in ancient folklore proves that it was generally known long before the beginning of modern times." It is clear that by the middle ages the sauna was important both in the routine life and the festivals of the Finns. "They went to the sauna every day to cleanse themselves; there they prepared for great festivals, and there they bathed before wedding ceremonies. . . . Many a child was born in the sauna and many an old man and woman carried there to die."[5]

Viherjuuri explains how the sauna was involved in the religion of the Finns:

53

The sauna was a place for the worship of the dead, who were supposed to return gladly, even after death, to so pleasant a place. . . . Some people believed that the throwing of water over the stones was a form of sacrificial ceremony. The Finnish word *loyly,* meaning the "steam which rises from the stones" originally signified spirit, or even life. . . . "In the sauna one must conduct oneself as one would in a church," according to an old Finnish saying. It was forbidden to make a noise or to whistle, or to speak indecently in a sauna, because all evil influences had been driven out.[6]

Although many of the old customs are no longer observed, the sauna continues to be regarded by the Finns with a certain reverence, a reflection of the ancient traditions.

It is interesting that the sauna seems to have evolved from the form of an ancient house of the Finnish-Estonian people. The sauna developed as a log cabin when the technique for building vertical walls of logs or boards was introduced to the northern forest lands of Europe. This sauna house replaced the previous pit house, a tepee-like structure, which has also been retained in Estonian custom as the summer outdoor kitchen. As building technology advanced, the Finns and Estonians adopted larger houses, but kept the small sauna house as an outbuilding used specifically for hot air baths.[7] It would seem that the early form of shelter became so strongly associated with its thermal function, to provide a warm place in a cold climate, that it was retained for an exclusively thermal use.

The fire of the hearth and the steam of the sauna were rather mysterious phenomena for our ancestors, which they explained in terms of their theory of how the world worked—a cosmology composed of spirits and gods. Fire and steam were valued because they were elemental. They offered an experience of the purity associated with the spiritual realm, and thus provided a link between the physical world of human beings and our ancestors' conception of the principles of the universe. Whether as a manifestation of a domestic hearth spirit or as a sun god, the fire was evidence of the powers of the spiritual realm.

We are not now inclined to regard modern heating and cooling systems as representative of a spiritual realm. The physical principles involved in their operation are thoroughly understood; there is no mystery about them. The air conditioner fitted into the window sash or the gas furnace in the basement are not thought of as expressions of a myth or as some metaphysical concept. They are simply functional, designed according to straightforward engineering practice to serve their intended function as efficiently and conveniently as possible.

And yet functionalism itself can be a kind of religion. It is part of the cosmology of a mechanistic universe where all objects and physical phenomena behave only according to objective principles. Building systems, machines, appliances come to be regarded as having a reality independent of human beliefs, their form and function determined solely by physical laws. They are all, however, most fundamentally, artifacts. They all have their origins in the human mind and therefore are inevitably formed by, and expressions of, the values, attitudes, and prejudices of their makers.

From the fifties and sixties we have inherited numerous heating and cooling systems created within an ethos of universal convenience. Machines to maintain our thermal comfort were conceived of as mechanical servants, providing for our every need while, like an English butler, remaining as unobtrusive as possible. Systems have been devised that can be given instructions by remote control or set to turn themselves on and off to maintain automatically the perfect thermal conditions. Portable unit heaters and air conditioners can be plugged in wherever a little extra warmth or coolness is desired. In addition to heating or cooling the air, appliances are available to exhaust stale air; to humidify it, so one's mucous membranes won't dry out; and to filter the air, so it will be free of all odors, dust, and pollen. The ideal seems to be a beneficent robot who will understand and meet all of its master's needs.

A striking contrast to the appliance approach to thermal comfort is seen in the ethos embodied in the design of passive solar-heated buildings. With the development in the United States of an ecological consciousness has come an attitude that we should not use technology to distance ourselves from the natural world; rather, we should strive for a more intimate, even symbiotic, relationship with natural forces. Solar design, especially in passively solar-heated buildings, provides a prime expression of these values and, thus, has come to be seen as a symbol of them.

Karen Terry's house in Sante Fe, designed by architect David Wright, is perhaps one of the most compelling passive designs. Stepping down its hillside site in four tiers, it nestles low into the ground. Thick adobe sidewalls create a strong sense of shelter and its banks of windows look resolutely to the sun. The image is very much of a house attuned to sun and earth. Rather than providing the convenience of a constant indoor temperature regulated by a thermostat, a passively solar-heated house may go through an air temperature flux as great as 20°F per day. People learn to live with this flux by putting on a sweater or moving to the part of the house with the most desirable conditions. Karen Terry follows the temperature changes in her house with a migration strategy similar to the Tunisians, who move through their courtyard houses according to daily and seasonal temperature cycles. She works in the cool lower level where she has her studio, eats in the middle level, and sleeps and bathes in the warmest upper level. She feels that the house, with its openness to the sky and its responsiveness to the climate, helps connect her to natural rhythms. "Living in a solar house is a whole new awareness, another dimension. I have the comfort of a house with the serenity of being outdoors—protected, yet tuned in."[8]

Janius Eddy, who lives in a solar home in Rhode Island, shares Karen Terry's sentiments. He describes the meaning his house has come to have for him:

> It is not just the financial savings. We grow more in awe of the tenuous hold our lives have on this small planet, more convinced that the sun renews us, in an almost religious way. It has made us profoundly grateful that the sun is up there, the center of our universe, warming us up and keeping us alive. That atavistic sense of the elements that early man knew and felt has become part of our lives.[9]

A solar house, geared to both the people who live in it and the cycles of the sun, is seen to exemplify the human relationship to the natural world.

Such an attitude is quite reminiscent of the ancients' fire worship as a celebration of the death and rebirth of the sun. It suggests a parallel between the symbolism of the hearth and of solar buildings. They both domesticate an elemental force to provide for pragmatic thermal needs. They both bring a primal phenomenon into the realm of everyday experience.

In addition to being invested with meaning in itself, a thermal system may also be used to reinforce the significance, or enhance the meaning, of other symbols. Interestingly, special thermal qualities are associated with symbolic places in many societies. Perhaps the provision of thermal comfort and delight is a way to emphasize the importance of the place for people. A simple example is the air conditioner in the boss's office. Along with the black leather chair and the deep pile rug, the air-conditioned office is a mark of executive prestige. The association of thermal comfort with status, as in the boss's office, seems to be a rather common pattern. The more expensive and difficult it is to provide thermal comfort, the more likely its use will be restricted to only those purposes deemed most important. Thus, in Saudi Arabia, if a family can only afford to air-condition one room, it is most likely to be the men's visiting room, the *ka'ah,* even though it is the room in the house used least frequently. Hospitality is an essential value of Saudi society, and so guests are given the best the family has to offer.

A mechanically cooled place is especially apt to be linked with symbols of status, perhaps because for so long excessively hot weather was considered inescapable. The heat was a great equalizer—something everyone had to endure, rich or poor, lowly or royal. While the problem of cold weather might be comparatively simple to remedy by building a fire or putting on an extra robe, the technology for countering hot weather was extremely complex and expensive. In medieval Islamic countries, incredible effort was expended to cool the throne or pleasure pavilion of the sultan. Elaborate waterworks were used to cool an area by evaporation. A prince in Alwar in India had his throne room in a marble pavilion that was "completely enclosed in a veil of spray falling from the cornice."[10] A similar approach was employed for the delectation of the Spanish sultan in Toledo: "In the center of the lake rose a water pavilion of stained glass adorned with gold. Here the sultan could recline in comfort on the hottest day, encircled by the glistening shower falling from the dome. At night tapers were lighted to glow through the transparent walls."[11] Regardless of how much benefit he actually derived from the elaborate system of cooling, it certainly added to the aura of power and privilege around the throne of the sultan.

The public baths of ancient Rome are an example of a thermal place that developed into an expression of the social ideals of a society. In early Rome, baths were a luxury found only in the houses of the very rich, those who could afford to finance the transportation of water over long distances and the cost of fuel to heat it. Entrepreneurs devised the idea of building bathhouses that would be opened to the public for a small fee. Such public baths, or *thermae*, became extremely popular, for like the Japanese baths they were both a social gathering place and an important source of warmth for the Romans. (Historians never fail to comment on the great thermal discomfort of the standard Roman apartment house, stuffy in the summer and unheatable in the winter.) The Roman statesman Agrippa, who as a young man had been a magistrate in charge of the public baths, conceived the idea of creating a free public bath. It was a grand egalitarian gesture, certain to make the government popular with the people. The Roman historian Carcopino describes it as "A revolutionary principle in keeping with the paternal role which the empire had assumed towards the masses."[12] Agrippa founded a bath to be free in perpetuity—named after himself, of course. Later emperors continued the tradition, each vying to construct the most enormous and sumptuous bath of all.

These *thermae* were among the wonders of Rome. No expense was spared in their construction and decoration. The finest marble, collections of ornate sculpture, and elaborate mosaic work combined to make the baths incredibly opulent. They were huge buildings with great domed spaces for the baths and many ancillary spaces for the other public uses incorporated into the complex. Carcopino describes how the spaces were used:

> Near the entrance were the dressing-rooms where the bathers came to undress. Next came the *tepidarium,* a large vaulted hall that was only gently warmed which intervened between the *frigidarium* on the north and the *caldarium* on the south. The *frigidarium,* which was probably too big to be completely roofed in, contained the pool into which the bathers plunged. The *caldarium* was a rotunda lit by the sun at noon and in the afternoon, and heated by vapor circulating . . . beneath the pavement. . . . To the south of the *caldarium* lay the *sudatoria,* whose high temperature induced a perspiration like the hot room of a Turkish bath. Finally the whole gigantic layout was flanked by *panestrae,* themselves backing on recreation rooms, where the naked bathers could indulge in their favorite forms of exercise.
>
> Externally the enormous quadrilateral was flanked by porticos full of shops and crowded with shopkeepers and their customers; inside it enclosed gardens and promenades, stadia and rest rooms, gymnasiums and rooms for massage, even libraries and museums. The

baths in fact offered the Romans a microcosm of many of the things that make life attractive.[13]

These *thermae* were also miracles of Roman technology that astound the visitor even today. The rooms were enormous and yet, contrary to one's intuitive expectation that such spaces would be drafty and cool, they could be kept extremely warm, even hot. The secret was in the use of a radiant system of heating that could warm a bather regardless of the air temperature. Hot fumes from a great central fire were channeled through hollow tiles within the floor and walls so that the bather was surrounded by surfaces radiating heat. This system was so effective that the baths at Ostia, fifteen miles west of Rome, could be built with great open windows; they were essentially open-air baths. The openings were all oriented to the south to take maximum advantage of solar heating. But even on a cloudy winter's day the heat radiating from the walls and floor was sufficient to maintain bathing, even steam-room, conditions.

The baths were a physical manifestation of the ideal that every Roman citizen was entitled to benefit from the wealth reaped by the empire. Carcopino writes, "In their dazzling marble grandeur the *thermae* were not only the splendid 'Palace of Roman Water,' but above all the palace of the Roman people, such as our democracies dream of today."[14]

Temples in India offer an intriguing example of the conjunction of a thermal place and a sacred place. The great stone temples of southern India, such as those at Madurai and Kancheepurum and many smaller temple towns, provide a sanctuary from the pervasive heat of the tropical climate, where the seasons are sometimes described as hot, hotter, and hottest. A visit to one of these temples will quickly convince the traveler that they are the coolest places to be found in southern India, except, of course, the air-conditioned international tourist hotels. Townspeople and pilgrims come to the temples for prayer and meditation, but often stay to take an afternoon siesta on the cool stone floors or even to conduct business along the deeply shaded arcades. While the rest of a traditional Hindu town is built of mud and thatch and wood, the use of stone is reserved for temples. It is used for the pyramidal structures that top the shrines (*vimana*) and gateways (*gopurum*) and for the columned halls and long arcades that enclose the sacred compounds. This enormous quantity of stone provides a thermal mass that never reaches the extremes of the air temperatures.

A cool town center, for both sacred and social uses, can be found in the traditions of the ancient Aryans. The villages of the Aryan tribes were centered around a huge tree that "symbolized the axis around which the universe and the celestial realms were believed to rotate."[15] It was in the cool shade of this sacred tree that the village elders met in the *panchayat,* or village council, and it was there that the children were instructed in the sacred texts. This shaded village center grew to include other communal and sacred functions such as a community dancing ground, a local shrine, and, very important, a well or open water tank.[16]

The tradition of the great shade tree as the sacred meeting place at the center of the village may have served as a model for the great stone temples that began to be constructed in the medieval period. Newly powerful Hindu rulers sponsored the building of the temples to form the nuclei of towns. Until the medieval period, Hindus had worshiped primarily at small local shrines and individual altars. These new temple compounds included not only the sacred shrine but the other more communal functions of the traditional Aryan village as well. There was a dancing hall, a temple tank for ritual ablutions, and a deeply shaded place for discussion and teaching of religious texts.

The stoneworking technology necessary for building the temples was late to develop in India. The earliest stone temples were not constructed; they were carved. The chaitya-halls, or prayer halls, of the Buddhists (ca.250–700 AD) were hewn directly into the face of rock cliffs. At Ajanta, thirty such temple-caves can be found along a single cliff wall. Monasteries were also carved out, using the form of a single-story wooden house built around an atrium, with rooms that open directly onto the court.[17]

The association of caves with religious pursuits is quite common, as Bernard Rudofsky points out: "Faith, piousness, and religiosity of all shading seem to thrive in their padded silence. . . . The basic cavern . . . with its dripping water and bone chilling drafts . . . is supremely qualified to induce a feeling of lightheadedness which furthers meditation."[18] Caves are the stereotypical home of the Christian hermit, along with the Buddhist and Hindu ascetics of India. Innumerable churches were carved into the ground in Ethiopia, Anatolia, southern Italy, and many other areas around the Mediterranean. The distribution of such cave retreats has a clear climatic component, however: they are found only in warm climates where the even temperature of a cave feels cool and comfortable, rather than consistently cold and uncomfortable as in northern caves.

The Buddhist chaitya-halls served as an important prototype for the first southern Indian attempts at stone temples. One early Hindu ruler is reported to have initiated a competition among architects to determine the best form for the Hindu temples that were to be built with the new technology of stone work. Buddhist chaitya-halls and monasteries, in addition to portable wooden shrines and reed-roofed houses, were used as models for the reduced-scale temples that were carved from a single ridge of stone that formed the competition site. These diminutive temples were left half finished, some columns carved in full detail and others left only roughly formed. The most successful model proved to be a square pyramid, a shape that satisfied all the formal, ritual, and cosmological requirements for Hindu worship.[19] It also effectively placed the sanctuary under a mountain of stone. The earliest temples, such as the shore temple at Mahabilipurum, consisted of this pyramid over the shrine, the *vimana*, surrounded by a low wall. Additional compounds were commonly added later in concentric rings, forming a rectangular mandala, each inner ring being progressively more sacred. With each ring a larger temple gate, or *gopura*, was added. The outermost *gopurum* are enormous and can be seen for miles across the plains.

The temple also included, in its architectural form, the means for being blessed by the four elements—earth, wind, water, and fire. Before entering the temple gates, one removed one's shoes to touch and be blessed by the earth. Then upon passing through the temple gateway, one is blessed by the air with a gust of wind. Villagers believe that the ancients knew how to use the magic of the winds to ensure that there would always be a breeze blowing through the gateway, and in a sense they did. The high pyramids over the gateways catch the slightest breeze aloft, creating a high pressure area that forces a turbulent wind through the narrow passage at ground level, in the same way that American skyscrapers create gusty wind problems at their bases.

A blessing by water is obtained by bathing in the temple tank, or at least descending its steps to touch the water and get a piece of one's garment wet. Finally, on entering the cool interior of the sanctuary, the worshipper is given a mark on the forehead with ashes taken from a small sacred flame by an attendant priest. Even this blessing by fire has a slight cooling sensation to it. Perhaps it is only coincidental that each of these four blessings is associated with a cooling sensation; and yet, the use of forms and materials that inevitably create coolness is quite remarkable.

Some mention should be made here of the role of the temple tanks. Their use is quite ancient, as evidenced by the excavation of tanks at Mohenjo-daro (ca. 2000 BC). It is presumed that, in addition to serving as a water reserve for the community, they were also used for ritual bathing, a purification rite common in India and many other cultures.[20] Similar tanks are found in India today, both within the temple grounds and along the roadside, often with a large banyan or other tree shading the water and the steps leading down to it, providing a cool wayside stopping place for the traveler. Some of the tanks or wells outside of the temple compounds have a sacred nature of their own. The step-well temple at Adjalaj in the northern Indian desert is an interesting example. The temple-well is built as a series of columned terraces that descend six stories into the ground to meet the variable level of the water table. The well serves as a gathering place for villagers who seek relief from the desert heat. They come to get water and also to worship. Ablutions are performed at each level of the step-well, as the villagers step down to the progressively darker and cooler levels, gradually approaching the water at the bottom.[21]

From these examples—Islamic thrones, Roman *thermae,* Indian stone temples—we can see places whose thermal qualities reinforce their significance within the culture. The thermal qualities may be operating at a level of necessity, like the Roman baths or Indian temples that use collective resources to make basic warmth or coolness available to the whole community. They may employ elements of delight, as do the pleasure pavilions of the sultans or the sensual blessings of the four elements in Indian temples. And they may enhance the attractiveness of a place as a social setting so that, like the Roman baths and Indian temples, they become social centers of the community. In all these ways thermal qualities enrich one's experience of a place and increase its value. Perhaps the simple bodily experience of thermal conditions is sensed as a metaphor for the more abstract meanings represented by a place: the comfort, the delight, the social affinity, each reinforcing the overall significance of the place in people's lives.

The integration of all of these aspects of a thermal place is perhaps most powerfully seen in the tradition of paradise gardens in Islamic countries. Here, the garden or courtyard has a very simple thermal function—to provide cooling with shade and breezes and evaporation from water and vegetation—and has also evolved into a complete metaphorical representation of a people's world view. There are two basic types of Islamic garden. One is the garden in the inner courtyard of a house, such as the famous gardens at the Alhambra in Granada, Spain. The Persian word *bustan* is used to describe these enclosed, formal gardens that constitute a basic formal element of Islamic houses from Spain to India. The second type is not nearly so pervasive but has had an enormous influence on the role of the garden in Islamic culture. It is the palace garden, or rather the *bagh,* an entity comprising palace and garden together.

Both the courtyard and the royal garden have very long histories in the middle east. Their forms are found in the ruins of some of the earliest urban settlements. We know that specially irrigated royal pleasure gardens existed at least as early as the sixth century BC when Cyrus the Great built his palace at Pasargadae in Iraq. Long porticos and a columned pavilion provided shade within the garden compound. A stone water course, with shallow pools at regular intervals, "was clearly the installation of a formal garden."[22]

It is quite understandable that for a desert people the garden became a metaphor for paradise. The Bible mentions the Garden of Eden, the paradise that existed on Earth, as the original home of humankind before the fall from grace. The Koran continued the tradition of Eden, assuming that it would also be our final home in Heaven. "Theirs shall be the gardens of Eden, underneath which rivers flow: therein they shall be adorned with bracelets of gold, and they shall be robed in green garments of silk and brocade, therein reclining upon couches—O how excellent a reward! And O, how fair a resting place!"[23]

To provide an image of its promised paradise, the Koran used descriptions of earthly pleasures such as might have been found in the royal pleasure gardens of the time. There shall be "two gardens, green green pastures, therein two fountains of gushing water, therein fruits, and palm-trees, and pomegranates, therein maidens good and comely . . . houris, cloistered in cool pavilions . . ." And, "Therein they shall recline upon couches, therein they shall see neither sun nor bitter cold, near them shall be its shades, and its clusters hang meekly down . . ."[24] In these passages it can be seen that the coolness of shade and water and lush greenery is one of the most essential attributes of this garden paradise. It sounds indeed like the paradise of a desert people.

The Koranic description of paradise became a guide to pattern earthly gardens after. The faithful hoped to create an anticipation of heaven with their gardens, and immodest rulers tried to build themselves a paradise on earth. "Islamic legend preserves the story of Shaddad, an ancient king of South Arabia, who attempted to rival Paradise by building the Garden of Iram in his kingdom. The story relates that a messenger was sent by God to Shaddad, warning him not to challenge the Almighty. When Shaddad ignored the warning, God destroyed the garden."[25]

The Koranic descriptions were carefully studied to determine the proper geography of Paradise so that gardens could be laid out in the same form. In one Koranic verse two gardens are mentioned with two fountains of running water, suggesting that paradise was made of two-times-two gardens. A fourfold division of paradise was also suggested by the four rivers mentioned in the book of Genesis that flowed out from Eden. The cruciform division of the garden by four channels of water that meet in the center became traditional throughout Islam. The significance of this form was reinforced by contact with Persian cosmology, as James Dickie explains:

> In Persian ceramics approximately datable to 4000 BC, the world—represented by a plaque or bowl—appears symmetrically divided into four zones by two axes forming a cross; at the point of intersection a pool is depicted: in other words, there at the focal point of the world the Spring of Life breaks the surface. This iconography, closely connected with the mandala of Buddhist iconography, expresses a vision of the universe, a life-symbol, which, by virtue of its adoption by conquering Arabs, was distributed throughout the entire extent of their empire. In this manner the Iranian garden came to constitute the prototype of the Islamic garden.[26]

While the parallel between celestial paradise and earthly gardens has ancient origins, the poets and religious teachers of medieval Islam were the ones who most elaborated on the metaphor. The Sufis, in particular, were fond of pursuing analogies between nature and the divine. The most benevolent aspects of the weather, the cool breezes and the rain, were identified with either God or the Prophet. The cool breeze was the Breath of God bringing his message of love, as words are carried on the breath of the speaker: "For mystical poets like Rumi, the appearance of the leaves in the spring is caused by their listening to the divine call *Alast*. . . . Moved by this word as manifested in the spring breeze, herbs and flowers come into existence in an enraptured dance." Rain is the symbol of Divine Mercy and is even commonly referred to as "mercy" by villagers and peasants.

> The life-bestowing activity of the rain is connected with that of the Prophet of Islam who was sent "as a mercy for the worlds"; hence we can understand the numerous poems which symbolize Muhammed as the "jewel-showering cloud," or as the rain cloud "pregnant from the ocean of love" which slowly wanders from Mecca to Istanbul and Delhi to quicken the dead gardens of the human hearts by his message.[27]

The Sufis especially delighted in using the garden as a metaphor for the human condition. The soil of the garden was identified with the mortality of human beings: "As the dead earth will be resurrected in spring to be adorned with lovely green sprouts and flowers, the dead bones of the true believers will be quickened again as they are allowed to enter paradise."[28] This link between the lives of owner and garden often continued literally after death. While the word *firdaus* stands for both garden and paradise, another word *rauda*, can be used interchangeably for garden and mausoleum.[29] In India there are many grand pavilions that now sit in the midst of barren pieces of ground, empty monuments whose only function is to shelter a sarcophagus. Elaborately carved stone screen-work, patterned marble floors, and airy vaults combine to make them wonderfully cool places. It seems a bit strange that so much effort was expended to provide thermal comfort for a sarcophagus. But at one time each structure was the pleasure pavilion of a king's garden. The Mughuls of India developed a tradition where each ruler commissioned his own garden. Then, "At the owner's death the pavilion, generally placed in the center of the site, became the mausoleum, and the whole complex passed into the care of holy men."[30] Thus, rather than passing from one generation to the next, the garden remained specifically for the one king. James Dickie writes: "The garden frequently served as a burial-place where the owner, inadequately satisfied with the pleasures it had given him whilst he lived, wanted to continue enjoying them even in death and where—symbolically—he had already entered into Paradise."[31]

The widespread religious imagery of the garden encouraged all owners, royal or common, to regard their gardens with reverence, as a continuing allegory of their relationship to God: as the garden prospered, so did the soul of the inhabitant. In the Sufi metaphor, the body of the owner is seen as the soil of the garden, as the place itself. Similarly, the life processes of the owner were reflected in all of the processes of the garden, not only the plants that grew and died every year but also the water running in channels and fountains, the breezes cooled by shade and evaporation, the sounds and smells of birds and flowers. The life of the garden and the life of the owner were tied together, one as an allegory of the other.

The garden, either as *bagh* or *bustan*, is as central to the concept of an Islamic home as the hearth is to the European home. It is interesting, then, that the hearth-fire in old traditions has a similar association with the life of the inhabitants of the house. Commonly, the fire of the hearth was not allowed to go out. It was carefully covered with ashes each night at curfew so that a few selected embers would survive until morning. (In fact, the word "curfew" originated from the French word for cover-the-fire—*couvre-feu*.) Raglan comments that "the alarm and horror felt if the hearth-fire went out are out of all proportion to the inconvenience caused" by the need to relight it. The fire was ritually extinguished and rekindled only on special occasions usually having to do with the death or, less commonly, the birth of a member of the household.[32] The Catholic Church absorbed this tradition into Easter ceremonies marking the death and rebirth of Christ: "On Easter Eve, it has been customary in Catholic countries to extinguish all the lights in the churches, and then to make a new fire. . . . At this fire is lit the great Paschal or Easter candle, which is then used to rekindle all the extinguished lights in the church."[33] The symbol of the eternal flame, which we use for our Olympic games and on the graves of presidents, would seem to have had a long history developed from the continuing hearth fire that represented the life and welfare of the residents of the house.

The connection between the life of the fire and the life of the inhabitant is also reflected in the custom of the housewarming ceremony. In contemporary America a housewarming party is given when a family moves into a new house. Perhaps all of the friends and their good wishes are thought to warm the house metaphorically. In traditional cultures, however, the warming is quite literal, for it involves the bringing in, or the first kindling, of the hearth fire, which then creates the proper spirit and sanctity to transform the house into a home:

> In ancient Greece the hearth or *hestia* was the centre of domestic life. At a wedding, fire was carried to the *hestia* in the new home by the bride's mother, thus ensuring the continuity of domestic worship. In India the newly wedded pair formerly brought to their own house a portion of the sacred fire which had witnessed their union and which, when kindled on their own family hearth, had to be maintained ever afterwards for use in all domestic ceremonies, including the last

ceremony of all, the final burning of their bodies after death. . . . In Wales even now cases are known, when a new household is being started, of carrying fire from the parent hearth.[34]

Aside from a religious rationale, we can easily imagine from our own experience why fire might be used as a symbol of the life of a house and the family that lived there. The fire was certainly the most lifelike element of the house: it consumed food and left behind waste; it could grow and move seemingly by its own will; and it could exhaust itself and die. And most important it was warm, one of the most fundamental qualities that we associate with our own lives. When the fire dies, its remains become cold, just as the body becomes cold when a person dies. Drawing a parallel to the concept of the soul that animates the physical body of the person, the fire, then, is the animating spirit for the body of the house.

Notes

Necessity

1   Ralph Knowles
Energy and Form: An Ecological Approach to Urban Growth
Cambridge MA: MIT Press 1974
page 11

2   James Marston Fitch and Daniel Branch
"Primitive Architecture and Climate"
Scientific American December 1960
page 138

3   Ibid.
page 136

4   Vitruvius
The Ten Books on Architecture
trans. Morris Hicky Morgan
Cambridge MA: Harvard University Press 1914
page 38

5   Baruch Givoni
Man, Climate and Architecture
Amsterdam: Elsevier 1969
page 50

6   S. Olesen et al.
"Comfort Limits of Man Exposed to Asymmetric Thermal Radiation"
Thermal Comfort and Moderate Heat Stress
Building Research Establishment Report #2
London: Her Majesty's Stationery Office 1973

7   Victor Olgyay
Design with Climate
Princeton NJ: Princeton University Press 1963
page 17

Delight

1   James Marston Fitch
    American Building: The Environmental Forces That Shape It 2nd ed.
    Boston MA: Houghton Mifflin Co. 1972
    page 46

2   H. J. Viherjuuri
    Sauna: The Finnish Bath
    Brattleboro VT: Stephen Green Press 1972
    page 22

3   Tetsuro Yoshida
    The Japanese House and Garden
    New York NY: Frederick Praeger 1955
    page 16

4   Kenneth Rexroth, trans.
    One Hundred Poems from the Chinese: Love and the Turning Year
    New York NY: New Directions Publishing Corp. 1970
    page 42

5   Yoshida
    The Japanese House Garden
    page 16

6   Yi-Fu Tuan
    Topophilia:
    A Study of Environmental Perception, Attitudes, and Values
    Englewood Cliffs NJ: Prentice-Hall 1974
    page 10

7   Ibid.
    page 8

8   Gaston Bachelard
    The Psychoanalysis of Fire
    trans. Alan C. M. Ross
    Boston MA: Beacon Press 1964
    page 14

9   Andreas Volwahsen
    Living Architecture: Islamic Indian
    London: Macdonald and Co. 1970
    page 92

Affection

1   John F. Embree
    Suye Mura: A Japanese Village
    Chicago IL: Chicago University Press 1964
    page 49

2   Norma Skurka and John Naar
    Design for a Limited Planet: Living with Natural Energy
    New York NY: Ballentine Books 1976
    page 130

3   John Summerson
    Heavenly Mansions and Other Essays on Architecture
    New York NY: Charles Scribner's Sons 1948
    page 2

4   Lawrence Wylie
    Village in the Vaucluse, 2nd ed.
    Cambridge MA: Harvard University Press 1964
    pages 145, 146

5   Ibid.
    page 146

6   Noriko Nishizawa, Japanese architect
    personal communication

7   Bernard Rudofsky
    The Kimono Mind: An Informal Guide to Japan and the Japanese
    Garden City NY: Doubleday & Co. 1965
    page 136

8   Ruth Benedict
    The Chrysanthemum and the Sword
    Boston MA: Houghton Mifflin Co. 1946
    page 178

9   Nishizawa
    personal communication

10 Embree
    Suye Mura
    page 93

11 Nishizawa
    personal communication

Sacredness

1 Yi-Fu Tuan
Topophilia:
A Study of Environmental Perception, Attitudes, and Values
Englewood Cliffs NJ: Prentice-Hall 1974
page 145

2 Lord Raglan
The Temple and the House
London: Routledge and Kegan Paul 1964
page 77

3 James Frazer
The New Golden Bough
ed. Theodor H. Gaster
New York NY: New American Library 1964
page 708

4 Ibid.
page 722

5 H. J. Viherjuuri
Sauna: The Finnish Bath
Brattleboro VT: Stephen Greene Press 1972
page 16

6 Ibid.
page 18

7 Kalev Ruberg
"Evolution of an Estonian Farm Vocabulary"
unpublished paper, MIT Department of Architecture

8 Norma Skura and Jon Naar
Design for a Limited Planet: Living with Natural Energy
New York NY: Ballantine Books 1976
page 76

9 Ibid.
page 130

10 C. M. Villiers-Stuart
Spanish Gardens: Their History, Types and Features
London: B. T. Batsford 1929
page 9

11 Ibid.

12   Jerome Carcopino
Daily Life in Ancient Rome
ed. H. T. Rowell, trans. E. O. Lorimer
New Haven CT: Yale University Press 1940
page 255

13   Ibid.
page 256

14   Ibid.
page 263

15   Ancheas Volwahsen
Living Architecture: Indian
London: Macdonald and Co. 1969
page 46

16   Anita Ray
Villages, Towns, and Secular Buildings in Ancient India
Calcutta: Firma K. L. Mukhopadhyay 1964
page 19

17   Volwahsen
Living Architecture: Indian
page 103

18   Bernard Rudofsky
The Prodigious Builders
New York NY: Harcourt Brace Jovanovich 1977
page 22

19   Volwahsen
Living Architecture: Indian
pages 137, 138

20   Edwin Oliver James
From Cave to Cathedral
New York NY: F. A. Praeger 1965
page 226

21   Klaus Herdeg
Formal Structure in Indian Architecture
Limited-edition monograph of an exhibition, Ithaca NY: 1967

22   Ralph Pinder-Wilson
"The Persian Garden"
The Islamic Garden
eds. Elizabeth MacDougall and Richard Ettinghausen
Washington DC: Dumbarton Oaks 1976
page 72

23   Koran, Sura 18/30

24   Koran, Sura 55/46–75, 76/12–22

25   William Hannaway
"Paradise on Earth"
The Islamic Garden
page 46

26   James Dickie
"The Islamic Garden in Spain"
The Islamic Garden
page 91

27   Annemarie Schimmel
"The Celestial Garden"
The Islamic Garden
pages 27, 28

28   Ibid.
page 26

29   Dickie
"The Islamic Garden in Spain"
page 91

30   Susan Jellicoe
"The Mughal Garden"
The Islamic Garden
page 112

31   Dickie
"The Islamic Garden in Spain"
page 91

32   Raglan
The Temple and the House
pages 77, 82

33   Frazer
The New Golden Bough
page 702

34   Raglan
The Temple and the House
page 78